DIALOGUES ABOUT GOD

New Dialogues in Philosophy

A series in dialogue form, explicating foundational problems in the philosophy of existence, knowledge, and value

Series Editor

Professor Dale Jacquette
Senior Professorial Chair in Theoretical Philosophy
University of Bern, Switzerland

In the tradition of Plato, Berkeley, Hume, and other great philosophical dramatists, Rowman & Littlefield presents an exciting new series of philosophical dialogues. This innovative series has been conceived to encourage a deeper understanding of philosophy through the literary device of lively argument in scripted dialogues, a pedagogic method that is proven effective in helping students to understand challenging concepts while demonstrating the merits and shortcomings of philosophical positions displaying a wide variety of structure and content. Each volume is compact and affordable, written by a respected scholar whose expertise informs each dialogue, and presents a range of positions through its characters' voices that will resonate with students' interests while encouraging them to engage in philosophical dialogue themselves.

Titles

J. Kellenberger, *Moral Relativism: A Dialogue* (2008)
Michael Ruse, *Evolution and Religion: A Dialogue* (2008)
Charles Taliaferro, *Dialogues about God* (2008)

Forthcoming Titles

Bradley Dowden, *The Metaphysics of Time: A Dialogue*
Dale Jacquette, *Dialogues on the Ethics of Capital Punishment*
Michael Krausz, *Relativism: A Dialogue*
Dan Lloyd, *Ghosts in the Machine: A Dialogue*
Brian Orend, *On War: A Dialogue*

DIALOGUES ABOUT GOD

CHARLES TALIAFERRO

ROWMAN & LITTLEFIELD PUBLISHERS, INC.
Lanham • Boulder • New York • Toronto • Plymouth, UK

ROWMAN & LITTLEFIELD PUBLISHERS, INC.

Published in the United States of America
by Rowman & Littlefield Publishers, Inc.
A wholly owned subsidary of The Rowman & Littlefield Publishing Group,
Inc.
4501 Forbes Boulevard, Suite 200, Lanham, Maryland 20706
www.rowmanlittlefield.com

Estover Road, Plymouth PL6 7PY, United Kingdom

British Library Cataloguing in Publication Information Available

Library of Congress Cataloging-in-Publication Data

Taliaferro, Charles.
　Dialogues about God / Charles Taliaferro.
　　p. cm.—(New dialogues in philosophy)
　Includes bibliographical references.
　1. God. I. Title.
　BL205.T35 2009
　211—dc22

2008019237

ISBN-13: 978-0-7425-5962-2 (hardcover : alk. paper)
ISBN-13: 978-0-7425-5963-9 (pbk. : alk. paper)
ISBN-13: 978-0-7425-6398-8 (electronic)

Printed in the United States of America

♾™ The paper used in this publication meets the minimum requirements of
American National Standard for Information Sciences—Permanence of Paper
for Printed Library Materials, ANSI/NISO Z39.48-1992.

In gratitude for the life and work of Roderick Chisholm (1916–1999), an ideal philosopher who combined independent, original thought with humility and a passion for dialogue. Often covered with chalk stemming from what can only be described as exercising with a blackboard during long seminars, Chisholm consistently promoted peership between himself and his students. He encouraged us to challenge him and each other with unpretentious good humor and a commitment to intellectual integrity.

CONTENTS

ACKNOWLEDGMENTS

I am deeply grateful to Dale Jacquette for inviting me to undertake these dialogues. The following have been invaluable in offering assistance on improving different drafts of this project: Tricia Little, Christopher Waters, Valerie Deal, and Elizabeth Duel. I am also deeply grateful to Graham Martin, Dan White, Amy Hutton, Nikolaus Giaguinto, Hillary Bouxsein, Matthew Baudino, and Chris Miller. I am grateful to Amanda Gibson for her excellent copyediting and Janice Braunstein for her assistance in the final stages of preparing the manuscript for publication.

The format and content of this book reflect the work of many gifted students who have taken a course with me—Philosophical Theology—over the last several years. There are too many to thank individually, but in addition to expressing my deep gratitude to all, I thank in particular Adam, Amy, Andrea, Tempest, Benjamin, Brendan, Brett, Caleb, Christian, Collin, Darren, David, Dylan, Elsa, Emmy, Grant, Hannah, Laura, Jonathan, Karen (a.k.a. Ms. Bennett), Kate, Kelsey, Kieran, Kirsten, Jay, Jess, Liz, Marissa, Mary, Megan, Mike, Mr. Dolan, Mr. Glenn, Ms. Crane, Ms. Holme, Ms. Wynn, Neil, Noreen, Paine, Pat, Peter, Philip, Russell, Sean, Sir Kristopher, Thaddeus, Timothy, Valerie, and Vanessa. The first draft of this book was written by Lake Michigan with the Polichs of Dover Street, to whom I am deeply grateful.

INTRODUCTION

Some Groundwork

The outstanding American philosopher Charles Pierce (1839–1914) was once told, "Charles, you don't sound very sure of yourself." He replied that this was one of the greatest compliments he had ever received. Part of what made Pierce outstanding was that he engaged in self-questioning, rarely, if ever, assuming that his current convictions were obvious or unassailable. He articulated important substantial theories about science, nature, mathematics, logic, love, and God, and yet he was always prepared to step back and survey those reasons that might be mustered against his theories. One of the most dramatic cases of balancing an attachment to one's own convictions along with detached self-questioning can be found in the work of St. Thomas Aquinas (1225–1274). His principal writing was structured around a series of questions. Prior to his own arguments, he often began with arguments for the opposite stance.[1] His brilliance can be measured, like Pierce's genius, by his ability to see how and why—despite his massive intelligence—he might be wrong.

I believe that self-questioning can be overdone. One of my philosophy professors used to say that the goal of philosophy is to replace inarticulate certainty with articulate uncertainty. He had a passion for trying to break down what he saw as the unthinking dogmatism of his students. And he preferred skeptics with great debating skills and huge vocabularies to those of us who struggled to articulate positive, constructive theories. In the end, though, a consistent skeptic needs to be skeptical even about skepticism, because self-questioning can get out of hand: an unhealthy self-questioner might wind up questioning why she is raising questions about questions and on and on. I depart from my old professor in thinking that the practice of philosophy can lead one to new, confident convictions. Even so, we do well to be open continuously to challenges and a healthy self-questioning.

Throughout the history of ideas, some of the best examples of self-questioning and inquiry have taken the form of dialogues. From Plato (428–348 BCE) and Confucius (551–497 BCE) to this series of dialogues published by Rowman & Littlefield, dialogue has been a natural format for proposing positions and then testing them with objections and counterarguments. Dialogue is such a natural model for formulation and testing that Plato described thinking as a dialogue or conversation within the soul.[2] I believe that the dialogue framework is especially well-suited for our central topic: God.

Religious belief and skepticism can be profoundly central to who we are. Belief or disbelief in God is rarely a purely cerebral matter; it can have a deep impact on one's values, emotions, and relationships.[3] For a skeptic to consider the merits of Christianity or for a Christian to consider the merits of atheism can seem like an individual considering whether he or she should become a different person. This was certainly the way it was for me. When I was an atheist, then an agnostic, and then a theist, each change felt like a complete, radical shift of identity, and in many respects I think this is an accurate account of what took place. But as I continue in my personal reflections, dialogues with others, and the practice of philosophy itself, the art of self-questioning that I find in Pierce and Aquinas seems to me of overwhelming importance. I often wonder if maybe my earlier atheism was right, or perhaps agnosticism is the most reasonable stance of all. Without such self-questioning, I believe any of our current beliefs would fall into mere conventions and habits.[4]

I have also come to appreciate that self-questioning and placing oneself in the position of "the opposition" in dialogue is a vital part of being in a community of inquiry, a community which can be, at its best, a fellowship of friends. So, in my view, debate between theism and atheism is best seen as a collective inquiry in which there are shared goals (all parties are seeking respectful, fair inquiry) and virtues (one should seek to empathetically and imaginatively see the same topic from alternative points of view, which involves careful listening, not interrupting the other person, not dominating the discussion, cultivating charity, and so on). All this amounts not just to being friendly, but also, ideally, to being friends. Hence, for me, while I do see the debate between theism, atheism, and agnosticism about God as an exchange that can be deeply personal and life-changing, it is an exploration among positions that can each be articulated powerfully; each stance calls for ongoing re-exploration rather than the decision of a matter that is settled once and for all by a blockbuster argument. Moreover, like all exploration in the natural world, some of the best explorations—whether in the Himalayas or to North and South Poles—have been done by friends, or at least by those with bona fide comradeship.[5]

This book is far from the first dialogue on God. Historically, the topic of God has been the most common subject of debate in philosophical dialogues. God features in the dialogues of Plato (most famously in the *Euthyphro*, the *Republic*, and the *Timaeus*), Augustine of Hippo (354–430), Anicius Manlius Severinus Boethius (480–524), Anselm of Canterbury (1033–1109), Henry More (1614–1687), Gottfried Wilhelm Leibniz (1646–1716), George Berkeley (1685–1753), David Hume (1711–1776), and others. For these extraordinary thinkers, inquiry into God's existence was one of the most important tasks we can undertake. They each held that whether or not God exists deeply impacts the meaning of our lives. For them, the very practice of *philosophy* (a term that means "the love of wisdom") requires them to consider whether or not there is a divine wisdom that fashions the world. This conviction drove their inquiries into the nature and purpose (if any) of the cosmos, as well as their investigations into how we should live. If there is an all-good God, how should you act when you believe that God calls you to resist the directives of your nation or ruler? If there is no God, is everything permitted?

Today, friendly dialogue about God is pivotal given the recent wave of books that tend to completely denigrate the "other side." Hostile language makes it increasingly likely that, instead of dialogue, the only exchange we will have will consist of two or more groups simply announcing what they each believe and offering an unsatisfactory explanation of why those who disagree with them are biased, undereducated, fearful, cowardly, vain, stupid, *etcetera, etcetera, etcetera.* During such times, historically, philosophers have sometimes used dialogue as the primary tool in diffusing hostility. I believe this was the intent of Plato and Hume, and it was also a key motive behind *Dialogue concerning the Two Chief World Systems* (1632), the masterful work of the great astronomer and philosopher Galileo (1564–1642). At a time when there was fierce debate over whether the earth or the sun was the center of our planetary system, Galileo did the most reasonable thing under oppressive conditions: he constructed a dialogue in which the reasons for and against each view could be aired and compared. While one may argue that it was a bit too slanted in favor of Galileo's endorsement of a sun-centered system and although, sadly, his book did not in his lifetime lift the condemnation of this work, the *Dialogue* did challenge contemporary church resistance to modern science and stimulate substantial further inquiry in the next and future generations. His dialogue (like those by the philosophers cited earlier) is an excellent model for intelligent, substantial arguments in an open-minded, calm context, void of threats or arrogant sarcasm.[6]

The dialogue of which this book is composed features four characters: Pat, Chris, Liz, and Tony. I have chosen "Pat" and "Chris" as simple, non-gender-specific names. Pat is a secular naturalist who believes that religious belief is scientifically discredited. He or she thinks that the belief in God is superstitious and morally dangerous. Pat holds that the world that is disclosed by the natural sciences (physics, chemistry, and biology) is the most fundamental reality. Psychology, sociology, and history reveal important truths about the world as well, but all such truth must ultimately fit into a system of natural, as opposed to supernatural or theistic, causes. Pat's philosophy of naturalism matches the following succinct statement by Simon Blackburn: "To be a naturalist is . . . to refuse unexplained appeals to knowledge of a Platonic order of Forms or Norms; it is above all to refuse any appeal to a supernatural order."[7] Chris, on the other hand, is a theist. He or she thinks there is an all-powerful, good, all-knowing, necessarily existing, everlasting Creator who is manifested in religious experience. Chris does not make "unexplained appeals" to mind and God, but holds that the existence of God is fundamental to the cosmos insofar as the very existence and continuance of the cosmos requires the sustaining creative power of God. Without God's creative power, the cosmos would cease to be. In Chris's view, the natural world would itself give us reason to believe there is a good, purposive, divine reality. Although a theist, Chris has not decided whether to become a practicing Jew, Christian, or Muslim, embrace a theistic form of Hinduism, or simply be a theist in his or her convictions but remain detached or neutral about specific religions. Chris does, however, think that all of these traditions are live options. The concept of a "live option" comes from the American philosopher William James (1842–1910), who was a deep admirer and, in some sense, a follower, of Pierce. In James's terminology, a live option is a thesis that is worthy of assent and action based on the thesis; "dead options" are only matters of idle curiosity and not worthy of practical and theoretical commitment.

By giving center stage to the debate between theism and naturalism, I hope to highlight the biggest and most longstanding debate about God in the history of ideas, especially since the modern era (which is customarily dated with the emergence of modern science in the seventeenth century). While there are non-theistic concepts of God, theism has had the largest following in the West. Theism and atheistic alternatives are also widely represented in the East, especially in debates between Hindu and Buddhist philosophers.[8] In the current philosophical literature, a secular form of naturalism like Pat's is definitely the most vigorous, well-represented alternative to theism.

"Tony" is agnostic: I chose the name to honor a friend who is currently an agnostic. He thinks that we cannot (or at least we do not currently) know whether theism or atheism is true. Some who embrace a form of agnosticism go on to conclude that if theism and atheism are equally plausible, then it is epistemically permissible for one to accept either. In this dialogue, however, Tony holds that if theism and atheism are supported by equally strong reasons, then one ought to refrain from accepting either. One should, instead, withhold judgment. The term "agnosticism" is derived from the Greek *a* meaning "not" and *gignoskein* meaning "to know." Agnostics hold that if we do not know the truth or falsity of whether or not there is a God, then we should be neither atheists nor theists.

Liz is someone who holds that there is something not quite right about the debate between theists, atheists, and agnostics. She believes that God is beyond logical discourse and human concepts. To subject God to our concepts and theories is to put God—the infinite, transcendent reality—in a box or, from a religious point of view, in a coffin. The name "Liz" was chosen because the character reflects the view of a friend named Liz.

I have not given my four characters elaborate personality traits or placed them in colorful, dramatic circumstances. But I hope they display enough personality so that the exchanges in this book may be seen as an engagement between persons and not just an abstract juxtaposition of impersonal, disembodied arguments. For example, true to most secular naturalists I know, Pat is tough-minded, placing a premium on clarity and science, and deeply opposed (intellectually and personally) to what she or he suspects is superstitious. In contrast, Chris is more capacious (whether this is the result of naïve, weak-minded gullibility, or of insight and intellectual maturity you must be the judge).[9] But however successful or unsuccessful I have been in portraying persons, I recommend being aware of how a philosophical outlook on God or any other substantial subject can bear on one's identity as a person or character. William James noted how different types of persons or personalities seem to match different philosophies. If he is correct, then a dialogue between persons with slightly different personalities may provide a more helpful introduction to the philosophical exploration of a subject than one that sees philosophy as altogether clinical and impersonal. I believe that acknowledging such a personal side to philosophy is liberating: it can help one see more deeply into what motives are in play in different arguments, and it can help one be more objective in one's own thinking. For I suggest that assessing a philosophical position involves critically comparing the credibility and clarity of *all* the reasons that can and should lead one to accept, reject, or remain uncommitted to a position. And these reasons can reflect one's personal orientation to the world. The extent to which one's personal orientation is philosophically illuminating is a topic that the characters take up in the final chapter.

The function of this text is to help foster your own dialogue. What you will find in this book is the fruit of many dialogues with students, colleagues, and readers of my other works. My hope is that it will lead you to write or record dialogues of your own. The history of recorded philosophy is relatively short; Socrates died only 2,407 years ago from the date of my writing this introduction. In geophysical terms, this time is infinitesimal. Perhaps *you* can develop new, unanticipated arguments to shed light on the topic of God and a host of other profound philosophical topics.

There are five chapters or conversations in this dialogue. The first sets the stage for what follows. Pat, Chris, and Liz are introduced. The second conversation consists of the defense and critical evaluation of the traditional concept of God. The third concerns four major arguments for God's existence, along with abundant counterarguments. The fourth conversation focuses on the nature of evil and the question of whether the existence of evil rules out the possibility of there being a good God. The final conversation looks into a series of topics that are important for current philosophy of religion. Might it ever be reasonable to believe in miracles? Or to believe in an incarnation of God as a human being? What is behind the belief in heaven and hell? Tony then comes on the scene to present a skeptical alternative to the positions of Chris, Pat, and Liz. After each conversation there are some questions for further reflection.

In keeping with my plea about the role of camaraderie in philosophy in general—but especially the philosophy of God—I conclude with the four characters as friends who do not agree to disagree. Rather, they agree to start over, to re-question starting points and end points. They plan to expand their inquiry into different religions and alternative conceptions of the world and the sacred. In angry, less collaborative exchanges in which egotism dominates, probably the most prized achievement is the Parthian shot. This is the unanswerable, devastating reply you deliver to someone, usually upon exiting a scene; the Parthian shot is ideally designed to shut down rather than to expand dialogue. It is named for the famous maneuver of the Parthian cavalry who would feign retreat and then turn around to shoot their pursuer with deadly arrows while all along speeding away at full gallop. The dialogue I present to you contains no Parthian shots (at least not intentionally). In my view, the best reason to have one dialogue is to have another. If there is a Parthian shot in your own conversations about God, then I suggest that (metaphorically) the best course of action is for "the victim" to pull out the nasty arrow, get up, and then ask the archer to dismount so that you might have a proper conversation. It is in this spirit that the dialogue of this book is decidedly open-ended. If you have suggestions as to how to improve or reframe such a dialogue, I welcome your input.[10]

NOTES

1. This practice was formalized as the fundamental method in scholastic philosophy.

2. See Plato's *Sophist* (263e) and the *Theatetus* (189e–190a). In Plato's *Phaedrus* there is a passionate defense of the superiority of verbal dialogue over and against writing.

3. See *Emotional Experience and Religious Understanding* by Mark Wynn (Cambridge: Cambridge University Press, 2005).

4. John Stuart Mill (1806–1873) argued forcefully in *On Liberty* that without the entertainment of contrary beliefs we risk losing sight of what we positively believe. I suggest further that if you have a belief, but no idea about what that belief excludes or leads you to deny, there is a sense in which your belief is highly tenuous and virtually formless.

5. See the *Oxford Book of Exploration*, edited by R. Hanbury-Tenison (Oxford: Oxford University Press, 2005).

6. Incidentally, and in support of my statements heretofore, Galileo's *Dialogue* is now considered one of the great classics in the history of science.

7. Simon Blackburn, *Ruling Passions* (Oxford: Clarendon Press, 1998), 48–49.

8. In terms of numbers, theistic religions also seem to involve the majority of self-identified religious persons in terms of the current world population. Reliable figures are hard to attain, but in the 2005 *Encyclopædia Britannica*, the world population was estimated as follows: Christianity 33.06 percent, Islam 20.28 percent, Hinduism 13.33 percent, Chinese folk religion 6.27 percent, Buddhism 5.87 percent, indigenous tribal religions 3.97 percent, and Judaism .23 percent. See the encyclopedia for further self-identified religious traditions or communities.

9. In setting up this contrast, I am drawing on my own experience and recent literature, but there is no necessary reason why Pat should be "tough-minded" or Chris "capacious." The roles or characteristics might be reversed. For the names of specific philosophers behind Chris, Pat, Liz, and Tony, see the afterword.

10. I make a plea for friendship in philosophy of religion in the concluding chapter of *Evidence in Faith: Philosophy and Religion since the Seventeenth Century* (Cambridge: Cambridge University Press, 2005). For an overview of the use of debate in philosophy, see "Philosophers, Red in Tooth and Claw," by Thomas Chance and Charles Taliaferro, *Teaching Philosophy* 14, no. 1 (1991), 67–76.

FIRST CONVERSATION

Launching a Dialogue about God

We are the inheritors . . . of a conversation, begun in the
primeval forests and extended and made more articulate in
the course of centuries. It is a conversation which goes on
both in public and within each of ourselves.

—Michael Oakeshott[1]

Alice was beginning to get very tired of sitting by her sister on the bank and of having nothing to do: once or twice
she had peeked into the book her sister was reading, but it
had no pictures or conversations in it, "and what is the use
of a book," thought Alice, "without pictures or conversations?"

—Lewis Carroll, a.k.a. Charles Lutwidge Dodgson[2]

PAT: Why not see this world as all that there is? Religion involves going beyond what can be tested scientifically or observed. What on
earth might count as establishing that there is a God? If God is some (supposed) nonphysical or incorporeal reality, God cannot be sighted visually,
or heard, smelled, tasted, or felt in any tactile sense. The very concept of
God seems, to me, to be confused. I can make sense of the idea that there
is a god who acts, thinks, and feels so long as I picture god as a colossal
Titan or, perhaps, a magical human being. That idea makes sense but it is
outrageously false, a crude form of anthropomorphism in which we human beings project or imagine some force greater than ourselves to protect us. Once you abandon such anthropomorphism, however, what do

1

you get? Does it make sense to think that a nonphysical, immaterial thing can act or feel or have intentions? This would be like the great case of nonsense in *Alice in Wonderland* when Alice wonders whether you can have a smile without a body: "Well!" says Alice, "I've often seen a cat without a grin: but a grin without a cat! It's the most curious thing I ever saw in my life." Similarly, a person or person-like being without a body is a peculiar absurdity.

I sympathize with some religious ways of life like Taoism and Confucianism when these are understood as affirming the sacred or awesome character of the natural world. You might say I have a kind of spirituality insofar as I value and find the world to be a source of wonder, but I see no need in going beyond the world to explain it or make sense of it.

When it comes to positing a Creator God, I suggest we make good use of Occam's razor: if you do not have positive reasons for positing some being (or thing or event of any kind), do not do so.[3] I see no point to positing a God, and lots of reasons not to, hence I conclude there is no God, and the natural world is all that exists. My atheism is not merely a *negative* position. "Atheism" literally means the denial of God (from the Greek *a* for "not" and *theos* for "God"). I affirm the denial of God in light of my *affirmation* of this complex, awesome natural world.

CHRIS: Let me begin with where you end. I, too, find the cosmos awesome. I am in awe that there is a cosmos of interwoven laws of nature, matter, and energy, that humans can engage in successful scientific inquiry, that there is organic life and animals—including humans—with sentience or sensations, desires, conscious reflection, the power to act, emotions, and moral values. But two things lead me to resist your Occam's razor. First, while I do not think God is a physical object and I agree that God cannot be observed with our physical senses, like seeing a volcano or whale, I believe we can and do have experiences of God. Yes, while some people have reported seeing God as a material being or quasi-material force (God has been experienced as an oceanic reality, for example), there is more widespread testimony to experiencing something transcendent, a holy or sacred reality that provokes in us awe and worship. I do not think all such reports of an experiential awareness of the divine are confused, the result of superstition and fear, or merely figments of the cerebellum. Although the experience of God is very different from repeatable visual observations of stable material objects, this is to be expected given the limits of human nature and what I believe is the unsurpassable greatness of God. Those who have studied religious experience across time and place, such as Evelyn Underhill, have built up an impressive, mutually supportive portrait of the numinous (full of awe) experiential testimony about the divine. While I do not subscribe to any formal religious tradition, I find an impressive convergence of testimony in classical Judaism, Christianity, Islam, and some forms of Hinduism that this holy reality is a powerful, knowing, purposive, good Creator. So, I am not so sure your Occam's razor works here because "God" may not be some theoretical posit beyond experience, like a quark or lepton. But I am also especially skeptical about your skepticism because of one of the things you mention: the success of science. The sciences succeed in genuinely explaining things and events within the world. Well then, what about the world—or the cosmos—itself? If there is a purposive, good Creator of the cosmos we can explain the very existence of the cosmos itself. Otherwise, you might be very good at explaining things *in the cosmos* but not *the cosmos itself.*

THE COHERENCE OF THEISM: AN IMMATERIAL GOD?

PAT: There is much for us to discuss! I will certainly challenge these reports of religious experience and the idea that the cosmos itself requires an explanation that goes beyond the cosmos. My deepest objection is the one you have not yet addressed: the incoherence of there being a transcendent, *nonphysical* being. All the terms we use to describe intention, purposiveness, thinking, and feeling presuppose physical embodiment. I know what it is for you to be a good person by observing your material behavior, but without material embodiment, what sense is there to personal characteristics or desires and other psychological properties? An analogy may be useful. We know what it is like to be outside a house because a house is an enclosed object in a broader environment. But asking us to contemplate God is like asking us to contemplate something outside the whole environment of space itself. I can form no idea of any such reality. This was the point of my *Alice in Wonderland* observation: the very concept of a smile (or grin) only makes sense with respect to having a face. Take away the face and there can be no grin. Take away the body, and what sense is left to the idea that a person is still thinking, feeling, and acting? A nonphysical God makes as much sense as a square circle. All the testimony in the world that people have experienced a square circle (an object that has four right angles and lacks four right angles simultaneously) will not remove the absurdity.

CHRIS: I agree with your last point. If we know that the concept of God is incoherent or impossible, the testimony to experience God cannot be straightforward evidence that there is a God. So I'll defend the coherence of the idea of God by challenging what seems to be your materialism—the view that all that exists is physical. You seem to assume both the sufficiency and necessity of material, physical embodiment: a grinning, embodied cat makes sense (as does a Titan), and a physical spacetime cosmos makes sense, but going beyond both falls into nonsense. I'll begin by contending that there is more going on with you and I (cats, too, but let's start with humans) than the physical. I do not think our psychological concepts of purposes, desires, and so on are reducible to mere bodily processes. You can have all sorts of bodily processes that appear to embody some given psychological property, a grin or smile that suggests friendship, for example, when nothing of the sort is going on. Someone's physiology and behavior may both indicate friendship and wide-awake compassion when really there is malice or perhaps no psychological life occurring at all; an apparently friendly person may turn out to be a zombie. By a *zombie* I do not mean the Hollywood version of the living dead, but a being that looks, acts, and is constituted the same as you and I but lacks consciousness and sensations. My initial point, then, is that bodily processes alone do not guarantee psychology. I could have a fully detailed understanding of someone's brain states and behavior and yet have no idea about their psychological life. Of course, brain states and behavior are deeply intertwined with psychology, but psychology involves more than brains and behavior. So, even in our own case, feelings, emotions, desires, and so on involve more than the physical alone.

PAT: I suspect you are working with a very narrow concept of what is physical. I grant that one may specify brain and behavior states from a standpoint which excludes psychology. I cannot know whether you are happy if all I know is derived from an MRI or PET scan. But if I know which brain processes correspond with pleasure and happiness, I can discover essentially your psychology by way of your physiology. Your zombie hypothesis is merely a science fiction nightmare. In reality, we do not think it is possible to have two identical physical bodies and different mental lives. If your case for the coherence of theism rests on the coherence of zombies, I think you are in trouble.

CHRIS: As it happens, I do think that zombies are possible and that entertaining challenging, alternative forms of embodiment can be illuminating. In reality, sure, we do rule out the possibility of the mental and physical being so disjointed, but the fact that we can imagine the physical without the mental is a clue that more is going on than what we find in the physical, organic foundation for psychology. Also, your appeal to *correlation* raises a major issue. Correspondence is not identity. When you see a brain process that causes a mental state, isn't this a case when one sort of thing (electrical neural activity) causes another sort of thing (psychological feelings)? After all, when you discover a match between the data of an MRI with mental states, don't you learn about something that is in addition to learning about cerebral blood flow and the general status of the 100 billion interconnected neurons that make up the brain? I believe your materialism has a hard time accounting for conscious, lived experience in humans and other animals. Because materialism is problematic about humans, you cannot use it as a reliable and certain instrument to dispatch theism as incoherent or impossible.

PAT: I believe I understand your strategy. I am maintaining that the traditional concept of God as a nonphysical and yet intelligent, conscious being is absurd, or at least utterly mysterious. Your counterargument seems to be that human psychology is also mysterious; if we are such mysteries, why object to the concept of God? But, in my view, we are not utterly mysterious. I see no reason to think that psychology is anything more than brain processes and behavior. Yes, the mere fact of correspondence does not—taken alone—establish identity, but *consistent, comprehensive correspondence* is evidence of identity. Consider an extreme example. Let's say you don't know whether Mark Twain is Samuel

Clemens (two names for the same person) but every time you see Mark Twain, you see Samuel Clemens. Eventually you should reasonably conclude that these names refer to the same person. In science we treat correlation as a sign of identity. If every time there is light, there is a form of electromagnetic radiation resulting from the acceleration of an electric charge, we have reason to identify the two. If every time a subject is in pain her brain state is X (where X stands for certain neurons firing), eventually one is led to identify pain with X. You may not literally see her painful feeling when you look at X but that's because you are not her; feeling pain is how X feels from the inside, so to speak. To deny identity here and stick with mere correlation would leave us to think water is merely correlated with H_2O or heat is correlated with mean kinetic energy, whereas these are both identity relations.

Contrast my view of persons with yours: I believe that the natural world as revealed by the natural sciences is fundamental. Psychological properties and brain properties emerge as natural biological events. You seem to think that natural processes give rise to something else, something that is beyond neurology. I treat all intelligent life as complex, physical organisms that use energy, reproduce, and so on. You are asking us to take the radical step of imagining intelligent life with none of this cellular constitution and natural properties. The God you are referring to is a *supernatural* reality and I propose that any movement beyond the natural world, whether this involves positing psychology (or consciousness or whatever) beyond the brain or a God beyond the cosmos, is not credible.

CHRIS: I prefer not to use the word "supernatural" to describe my position because of its association with the term "superstition" (which by definition involves irrational belief) and I am reluctant to think that God is unnatural or beyond all that is natural. "Theism" is my preferred term (originating in seventeenth-century England) to refer to the belief in an all-powerful, all-knowing, all-good, necessarily existing Creator of the cosmos. Most of us theists believe that God has a nature—the divine nature includes omniscience or supreme knowledge, for example. But if by the "natural world" you mean the world described and explained by the natural sciences, then I do think God is beyond the natural world. God is not in the domain of physics (God is not a macro- or microparticle), chemistry (God is not a physical compound), or biology (God is not an animal or plant). I believe God is omnipresent (everywhere) in ways I can explain in our next conversation, but God's presence is not akin to the presence of a gas, solid, or liquid. And you are right—I think conscious, psychological states do share a modest similarity with the divine insofar as our conscious beliefs, desires, experiences, and so on also go beyond what may be described and explained by physics, chemistry, and biology.

I have serious reservations about your analogies. There is a profound difference between the mental and the physical that is not matched in your case of Twain = Clemens, light = radiation, water = H_2O, and heat = mean kinetic energy. In these four cases one may see and fully grasp the identity either in terms of composition (water *is composed of* H_2O) or identity of properties (Twain and Clemens are the same height and weight, wrote the same books, and so on). But in psychology—in our desires, feelings, and sensations—there is the overall property of *subjective conscious experience*. By observing your brain one may well observe the activation of networks of neurons, but one will never observe the subjective conscious experience itself. Similarly, by studying how I feel right now—focused, and engaged in reflection with you—I do not ipso facto study my neurological states. In our own cases, I suggest, we discover the reality of consciousness directly by simply being attentive to our experiences. In our scientific inquiry we then discover various correlations, but not identity. In brief, a neurological event (an event involving neurological processes) is distinct from the mental event (my thinking about God) to which it is correlated. Your suggestion that I do not see your sensations because they are only felt "from the inside" attempts to glide over the radical distinctness of sensations and brain activity. Your sensations are real, and if you claim that a given sensation *is* a brain activity, then when I see or touch one, I see or touch the other. I might complain that I do not see you when, actually, you are *inside* a house and there are no windows. But in principle I can go into the house or you can come out, while no close examination of the brain yields a direct examination of your sensations.

Maybe we can make progress by a slightly different line of reasoning. Let me grant for the sake of argument that human consciousness *is* a brain state (a view that I believe is demonstrably false). Will you nonetheless grant me that there is a difference between *the concept of consciousness* and *the concept of brain states and other physical phenomena*?

PAT: Well, I think that in the future we will eventually merge the two so that our concept of the brain will include the concept of consciousness. One concept will eventually absorb the other in a complete natural science. What follows if I allow that the concepts are distinct now?

CHRIS: Our first disagreement is over whether the very idea of God makes sense, with you holding that the very concept of nonphysical intelligence is like a square circle. But what I propose is that we currently have a durable concept of human consciousness which may (I am granting for the sake of argument) turn out to be necessarily physical, but does not preclude there being other forms of consciousness that are nonphysical. Unlike the square circle analogy, let me introduce an analogy of squares and rectangles. While every square is necessarily a rectangle, not every four-sided figure is necessarily a square. Similarly, while it may be that human consciousness is necessarily physical, it does not follow that every form of consciousness is necessarily physical. The concept of *nonphysical consciousness* is no odder than the concept of a rectangle that is not a square. What I am questioning is whether you can be so sure that if it turns out that human consciousness is a matter of cellular constitution, you can know that this is true of all possible forms of consciousness. We human beings are, after all, simply one form of life in a solar system which is part of a galaxy with 300 billion stars, and our galaxy may be only one of 100 billion other galaxies. You object that I am being anthropomorphic in imagining a conscious, nonphysical, transcendent reality, but I think it may be you who is being more anthropomorphic if you insist that any other form of consciousness anywhere must conform to the limits of human and other terrestrial life-forms. Pat, you should watch more *Star Trek*.

Let me summarize my position. Our concepts of action and desire can be quite distinct from our concept of physical or material realities. When I think mathematically or when I appreciate our friendship, I am not thinking of any brain events or processes that are involved in those activities. So, while I need a brain to think and act, the *concepts* of thinking and acting do not demand that the subject who thinks and acts must have a brain or corporeal body. In your earlier case from *Alice in Wonderland*, the very concept of a smile depends on the concept of a face, but with psychological properties and concepts there is no conceptual necessity of material embodiment. Switch the example from smiles to happiness. Yes, a happy human being is a happy vertebrate, but we can imagine all kinds of different possible forms of life where there is happiness without vertebrates. In fact, some cognitive psychologists today even claim that machines can think and have emotions. I do not believe that machines do think (for reasons we can take up on another occasion), but I believe that the claim by some cognitive psychologists makes sense. It is possible that machines which are not biological organisms could at some point be happy and think, even if currently they never do.

I suppose my point can also be made in terms of the power of our imagination. I believe we can imagine an intelligent purposive reality both inside and surrounding the cosmos, whereas you think we cannot. Of course, we can be mistaken in using our imagination. I might imagine that there could be time travel, but then it turns out to be impossible. In the case of God, I suggest that I along with billions of other people can imagine or conceive of there being a God and there is no reason to believe that this is like imagining an absurdity like a square circle.

PAT: You are right to note that our disagreement may stem from our use of the imagination. Your use of imagination strikes me as more a matter of fantasy. In fairy tales I can picture a frog turning into a prince, but surely this involves picturing a very different world than ours, a world of magic. I agree that when I act I do not picture and intentionally bring about brain events that in turn bring about muscle movements, and so on, eventually leading me to move about. But I do not know what it might be like for me or any other being to move about in the world without a brain, nerve endings, and muscles. Once we discover human anatomy we discover that certain things cannot take place. Maybe in some very abstract, remote sense, it is possible there can be disembodied agents or ghosts, but this is a radical distance from the actual world. All the minds and agents I see and picture in *our* world are embodied. We do not have a single reported case of intelligent disembodiment. Sure, stories can be told about zombies and ESP, but this tells us more about human creativity than about nature itself.

CHRIS: First, a modest point about frogs and princesses. According to contemporary physics, physical reality at the micro-level is homogeneous with respect to kinds of macro-objects like a frog or human body, so it is possible (however bizarre and not feasible through human technology) to so alter the micro-constituents of a frog body to make a tiny human being.

But putting such fantastic possibilities to one side, when it comes to a broadly conceived theism there is widespread testimony in which many people across time and cultures at least appear to encounter a transcendent, intentional, nonphysical reality. These may be controversial, but they are extensive and, unlike reports of square circles or smiles without faces, they appear to disclose a living, sacred reality. Moreover, the experience of the divine does not seem at all akin to voodoo zombies or paranormal phenomena. We are not limited to the Brothers Grimm fairy tales about frogs and princes. We have instead what seems to be comprehensive testimony of the experienced reality of the divine. But rather than press further the claims of religious experience now, consider cases of reported disembodied agency: cases of people having near death experiences (NDEs) and out of body experiences (OBEs). These are cases when, from a clinical perspective, a person's body fails and yet the person reports leaving their body, sometimes observing their body from a long distance away.

PAT: All these experiences can be accounted for on perfectly natural scientific grounds. Trauma to the brain generates hallucinations. We are making progress in identifying the relevant brain states using functional magnetic resonance imaging (FMRI).

CHRIS: I do not deny there is a neurological account of these experiences, but my point is different: What are reported in these experiences are states of affairs that at least *appear to be possible*. They are not like reports of there being a square circle—an evident absurdity, for no single two-dimensional object can both have and not have four right angles. Let us agree that no OBE is a genuine case of a person actually having experiences outside his or her body. Narratives of OBEs nonetheless seem coherent and presumably a scientist would want to take them seriously as possible occurrences even if we dismiss them as false in the end. OBEs are an example of the *coherence* of non-embodied agents.

PAT: Let me try one other line of reasoning that threatens the very coherence of your idea of God. Our ordinary concept of ourselves in the world is thoroughly embodied. I do not locate myself in the world from some detached point of view. Instead, I experience myself as a feeling, thinking, acting body in relationship with other bodies in a larger environment. Gradually each of us gets a broader and deeper concept of ourselves in relation to one another. In contrast, consider the oddity of a theistic God. Supposedly, God has limitless knowledge. How is that even imaginable? We seem to fall into nonsense with the concept of *disembodied knowledge*. All knowledge is shaped from having a specific, material life and point of view. Even maps—which seem like objective representations of the world—presuppose a point of view. When I see a map of the USA I am seeing a landmass as it would look to me if I was in the stratosphere and the earth was flat. My argument, put succinctly, is as follows: An omniscient being (by definition) is all-knowing. If a being has knowledge (whether this is partial knowledge or all knowledge) this is fundamentally based on embodied cognition. If God exists, God is disembodied. Therefore there cannot be a disembodied, omniscient being.

CHRIS: Two points in reply. First, I prefer not to use the word "disembodied" of God. "Nonphysical" will do. "Disembodied" suggests that something was once embodied and then lost it.

PAT: That is part of my point, though. Language about God is derived from language we use about us, namely *embodied* beings. But once you take away embodiment, you have stopped making sense.

CHRIS: Okay, let's keep your term "disembodied" for the moment. My second point is to challenge your portrayal of embodied knowledge. I suggest that our grasp of ourselves requires all sorts of interrelationships with others. Some psychoanalysts believe that your first primordial understanding of yourself is achieved by a parent or caregiver who enables you to see yourself as a subject with needs, appetites, desires, powers of motion, and so on. You come to know where and how you are from multiple perspectives that go beyond your own embodiment. In fact, coming to realize the reality of other people and their feelings involves imagining or picturing how the world looks to them. William James plausibly described infant awareness of the self and the world as a boom-ing, banging, confusing—essentially a boundless—mental realm. What you describe as embodied knowledge is something only achieved grad-ually as we locate ourselves from different points of view, grasping how we look to our parents, and so on.

PAT: But keep in mind: we may be able to integrate and imagine multi-ple perspectives and yet these perspectives are each had by embodied persons, not disembodied spirits or ghosts.

CHRIS: That is what I am challenging. I think that as we build up a con-cept of ourselves in the world we do so by thinking of ourselves from multiple points of view that could (for all I know) be had by a non-physical (or "disembodied") spirit or ghost. Don't we think about what the earth was like before any humans came into being? We do not seem to be talking nonsense when we adopt what might be called "a cosmic point of view," according to which the earth is a tiny planet in relation-ship to the whole of the known universe.

PAT: All talk of "points of view" (in my opinion) seems to still achieve its sense or meaning in relation to embodiment. Strictly speaking, a cos-mos cannot have a "point of view" so any talk of a "cosmic point of view" is strange. The whole point of cosmology is for us human beings to achieve an understanding of the universe, but such science is carried out by embodied human persons.

CHRIS: Yes, and yet these embodied persons are developing points of view of when there were no embodied persons. I even suggest there is a sense in which scientists might be said to be seeking a "God's eye point of view" of the cosmos, a view from everywhere. To summarize my second point: Our knowledge of ourselves and the world involves the power to transcend our limited, individual, bodily life, and to see ourselves in relation to other peo-ple, societies, other animals, the earth, and on and on. All these broader and multiple perspectives hint at what would be known by an omniscient God not limited to any one physical body.

PAT: I will argue against such possible disembodiments later when we discuss whether we human beings, and perhaps some other animals, can have an afterlife, and I will also challenge your claims later about religious experience. For now let me address your point about explaining the cosmos itself:

GOD AND THE EXPLANATION OF A COSMOS

PAT continues: I suggest that when you try to account for the cosmos as a whole, you're making a conceptual mistake. Yes—as a scientifically oriented thinker, I propose that everything in the cosmos can, in principle, be explained by other events and laws within the cosmos. But once we have explained everything within the cosmos, should the cosmos itself have an explanation? To think that there must be some overall super-explanation of the cosmos would be like arguing that if every person on earth has a mother, then all people together must have a Super-Mother.

CHRIS: Not quite. Being a mother is a biological ancestral relationship that makes no sense when we infer from the fact that each person has a mother to the existence of a Super-Mother. But an explanation of a thing's existence is different. The natural sciences work on the premise that the things in the cosmos can—and should—be explained in terms of other things. No matter how complete our explanations within the cosmos, we still need to explain why the cosmos exists at all, or why *this cosmos exists* as opposed to *some other cosmos*. My reasoning from parts of the cosmos to the whole is a matter of arguing that if each part of the cosmos is contingent (explained by virtue of other events) then the very cosmos itself is contingent. To account for why this contingent cosmos exists we must seek an explanation in a non-contingent reality—something that is not dependent for its existence upon anything else.

PAT: Setting aside the possibility of religious experience, the problem I have with this reasoning is that you are moving beyond all observation. How many universes have we observed being created and sustained by God? Or being caused by something extra-cosmic? Explanations within the cosmos make sense, but appealing to an extra-cosmic, unobservable thing does not.

CHRIS: I think we are currently observing a cosmos created and conserved by God, though my full argument for this will take shape later.

PAT: If you are correct about there being a Creator, yes; but we cannot or at least do not observe the creating and conserving. Let me advance my basic worry in another fashion. Maybe you do have a good argument—I am skeptical—but isn't the appeal to "God did it" or "God explains or can explain the cosmos" suspicious on the grounds that it is too easy? We haven't established—so far in our conversation—a very specific idea of God. Consider the following problem: let's say you are able to explain the cosmos by appeal to God. How is God's existence supposed to be explained? Do you need another God beyond God to create God? And then you are onto an infinite regress of causes.

CHRIS: Actually, let's focus our next exchange on all the divine attributes. I think a robust concept of God is defensible, but let me speak immediately to the so-called ease of appealing to God. The very concept of God in the main theistic religions of the world (classical Judaism, Christianity, Islam, and some forms of Hinduism) is of a reality that exists necessarily. God cannot but exist; that is, God's existence is not something that is or could be due to the causal power of any law of nature or God beyond God.

PAT: What could it possibly mean for God to exist necessarily? If God is not created by another God, do you suggest that God is somehow responsible for God's own existence? But that is impossible. If God created God, then God would have had to exist before God existed. Consider an analogy: for me to create myself, I would have had to exist before I did the creating. Neither I nor God can self-create.

CHRIS: Right. I do not think God created God, but I am proposing that the very concept of God is the concept of a being who exists necessarily. Existing necessarily is not, I suggest, some odd opaque property. I think there are necessary truths such as the law of identity: A is A, or *everything is what it is, and not something else.* The law of non-contradiction is necessary (A is not not-A), and so are the truths of mathematics ($1 + 1 = 2$ is necessarily the case); essentially $1 + 1 = 2$ is equivalent to $1 + 1 = 1 + 1$, which is an identity statement. In my view, God is not a number or a necessarily true statement, but like numbers and necessarily true statements, God's very existence, or *nature*, is necessary.

PAT: I have my doubts about these so-called necessary truths and the analogy with God, just as I have doubts about your earlier analogy between God and consciousness. Isn't it far simpler to see necessary truths as simply features of language? To say "A is A" or "everything is itself" seems to be saying something about us and the way we use the word "God"—for example, we might only apply the word "God" to a reality that is uncreated and not the effect of laws of nature and so on. But all that is about our use of terms rather than reality itself. In doing so, we set up necessary relations with language, but we do not thereby encounter necessary realities in the world.

CHRIS: What worries me about your proposal is that you seem to leave unexplained the necessity of your necessary laws of language, and unexplained the apparent independence of necessary truths quite apart from language. Consider linguistic rules: We do not merely arbitrarily or conventionally decide that "A is A" or "everything is itself." We simply cannot do otherwise. If I say "A is not A" I have not said anything unless we suppose that one of our terms "A" means something different from my other use of "A." So, I might say "girls are not always girls" if I mean by the first term "young females" and the second "the way young females usually behave." So, then, I might mean: young females do not always act the way young females usually do. That makes sense. But without this shifting around, the statement "young females are not young females" is nonsense or, if sensible, necessarily false. Apart from that, it certainly appears that if there were no language-users there would still be necessary truths as with mathematics or geometry (squares are four-sided) or formal truths like *it is impossible that there be more red balls than red round balls* and so on. Necessity is a feature of certain truths about reality, both in mathematics and the philosophy of God.

PAT: I still see all your examples as reflections of how we use terms like "balls," "squares," and the terms of mathematics. My overall point is that you make no progress if you simply define "God" as a necessary being and then bring in God to account for a contingent cosmos. Why cannot I simply define "cosmos" as necessarily existing?

CHRIS: Because the cosmos simply is contingent. There is nothing about matter and energy that gives us reason to think either or both (some think matter is simply "frozen energy" and thus, basically, only one kind of thing) are necessary. We can imagine that our cosmos did not exist at all, or imagine that there was some radically different universe or chaos. It is partly a belief in the contingency of the cosmos that fuels scientific inquiry. We need to use observation and theory to describe and explain parts of the cosmos because the parts could have been otherwise.

PAT: I am not so sure. Ideally our observations and scientific theory can give us explanations that (in my view) could not be otherwise, given our overall understanding of the natural world. Before we examine the nature of light and matter and energy in general, it may seem quite contingent that light travels at 299,792,458 meters per second rather than twice as fast. But an ideal theory will explain why light cannot be otherwise.

CHRIS: Such interconnections of laws can generate a conditional or relative necessity, but it is still, I suggest, a contingent cosmos. That is, if you set up a model of the universe and keep certain factors constant—the nature of light, electricity, and so on—then certain truths such as the upper limit of the speed of light follow. But you do not thereby provide any reason to think that the cosmos itself is non-contingent. Why is there light or any energy and matter at all? Or why could not the cosmic constants we discover have been different?

PAT: You believe there is a God—okay. But can't you conceive of the possibility that there is no God? As such, the "reality" you seem to be invoking with the term "God" seems just as contingent as the cosmos.

CHRIS: I certainly grant that theism might be wrong, and you may be right about atheism. From the standpoint of my limited knowledge, it is possible God does not exist. But if God exists, then God's nonexistence is not (in fact) possible. In reply to your line of reasoning, please note that I am not taking arbitrary concepts or terms like "God" and attaching the terms "necessarily existing." Rather, I am proposing that to conceive of God is to conceive of a reality that exists necessarily. So, if I am right, I cannot conceive of a necessarily existing being not existing.

PAT: We need to talk about God from the beginning. I think your concept of God is still a hodgepodge of anthropomorphic attributes with "necessary existence" tacked on. Can you coherently relate the different divine properties of necessity, knowledge, goodness, and so on? It seems to me that if we can imagine any divine being at all, we can conceive of lots of different ones. Why think "God is all-good and all-powerful" rather than "God is not good at all" or "God is perfectly good but only of limited power"?

INTENTIONAL AND NON-INTENTIONAL EXPLANATIONS AND TWO FRAMEWORKS

CHRIS: I am ready for conversation two, but I do want to highlight a general point we may both agree to. Despite the diverse models of the divine, they all are part of what may be considered intentional or purposive accounts of the cosmos. At base, God or all these gods are intentional, purposive beings, whereas, at base, your understanding of the cosmos is fundamentally impersonal, non-intentional, and non-purposive. Part of my task in our dialogue is to argue that it is more reasonable to accept an intentional account of reality than a non-intentional one.

PAT: Let me clarify my stance just a tad. I think there is intentionality and purposiveness in the cosmos; namely, I think humans and many nonhuman animals have intentions, purposes, and goals. But you are right, I do not think the cosmos exists as a result of any cosmic or transcendent intention, purpose, or goal. Purposive creatures like you and me emerged from causes that are not themselves purposive in that the causes had no prevision of the end they were bringing about. I suppose that is what I find so wondrous about the cosmos, the emergence of complexity and life from simple, lifeless components. My position, in contrast to yours, is that this amazing natural world of ours has produced intelligent conscious life without requiring any extra-cosmic, non-natural, or supernatural (or theistic) reality. The reason why I persist in thinking of your position as anthropomorphic is that you seem to think that to account for the cosmos you need a being unlike us—nonphysical, non-contingent, more knowing, powerful, good, and so on—but still like us.

CHRIS: Keep in mind, however, how anti-anthropomorphic I have been. I do not think that purposive, conscious reality must conform to human structures. The divine reality that I recognize and will explore with you philosophically is radically different from any carbon-based life-form. God is also (in my view and the view of most theists) maximally excellent or unsurpassably good. Most theistic traditions conceive of God as worthy of the highest praise, and this fundamental praise-worthy nature of God is what helps shape our understanding of God. All the attributes of God, like being all-knowing, all-powerful, necessarily existing, and so on, are great-making properties. So, what would be greater: *an intentional being with limited knowledge* or *unsurpassable knowledge? An intentional being with unsurpassable knowledge and highly limited power* or *an intentional being with unsurpassable knowledge and power? An intentional being with unsurpassable knowledge, power, and contingent existence* or *an intentional being with unsurpassable knowledge, power, and necessary existence?* We believe that each question reveals a layer of values in which we come to a greater understanding of God possessing what some philosophers call the greatest compossible set of properties. Two properties are compossible when they can be instantiated by the same object; so, *being omnipresent* is not compossible with *being a finite physical object*. Among the many reasons why we theists hold that God is nonphysical is if God were a finite physical object, God would not be omnipresent, and we think *being omnipresent* is an excellence; we also think all physical objects exist only contingently and this is not compossible with *existing necessarily*, which we see as an excellence.

PAT: I look forward to challenging this whole array of divine attributes or properties! Let me try one objection now, however, about this framework. You seem to be treating existence itself as a property, like being knowledgeable. But *existence* does not seem to be the sort of thing that can be used to define an object. Imagine I tell you I would love a cup of coffee now. I might add that I would especially like French roast. And yet if I added I want an *existing* cup of coffee, I would rightly be considered very weird.

CHRIS: Personally, I would love to get you an existing or actual coffee rather than a merely possible one! In my outlining the idea of God's maximal excellence I did not mean to suggest God has the property of existence or be-ing, but *being necessary* as opposed to *being contingent*. And these seem to me to be coherent, meaningful properties. I am a contingent being (or, to put it differently, I have the property of being contingent) for I might not have existed. But if God exists, God would be necessary and not contingent.

GOD AND LOGIC

Liz: Hold on, you two. Before you go any further, I need to register a protest. The "God" both of you are debating is too anthropomorphic. It is also too quasi-scientific. Give me a few minutes to explain. I suggest to you both that the concept of God is not as neat as you, Chris, sug-gest, or as crude as you, Pat, propose. God is beyond all human concepts and categories. That is why it is inappropriate to think of God as a non-physical person. Chris's categories wind up reducing God to a mere thing among other things. But Pat also winds up misunderstanding God. I suggest that if Pat is to recognize God, that "God" will have to be like some kind of physical thing or some reality we posit in physics, chem-istry, biology, or perhaps mathematics. But God is on an altogether dif-ferent order of reality. In a sense, I rather like Pat's analogy of the house and the cosmos. From the standpoint of human language, God's exis-tence does not make sense. But what else did you expect? God is not a tame, domestic animal to be controlled by human categories.

Pat: I welcome Liz to my side. I agree with her that the concept of God transcends logic and insofar as logic cannot apply to God, neither can thought. If logic, thought, or ideas can make no sense of God, then the concept of God is nonsense and God cannot be believed in, trusted, prayed to, worshipped, or even spoken about. I see this conclusion as es-sentially my own: the assertion there is no God.

Liz: You deny God. And I deny any God that is describable in human terms. God cannot be described; God is ineffable. Let me distinguish our positions. I believe that while God cannot be described, God can be ad-dressed. We can use language to speak *before* God or *in the presence of* God. I also commend a sacred silence before God in full awareness of the limits of our thoughts and categories. I further believe in living a life worthy of God by acting with justice, mercy, and compassion toward others. I am drawn to the more mystical dimensions of the great world religions. So, I am drawn to Maimonides' great path of negation in Judaism; I like mystics such as St. John of the Cross in Christianity; I am most at home in the Sufi tradition in Islam; and I love the Veda's portrait of Brahman as beyond our best language in Hinduism.

In my view, the whole point of thinking about God is to think about how to live our lives with reverence. The point is not to explain the cosmos or treat religious experience as evidence of a transcendent reality.

CHRIS: Actually, I think that your stress on the role of belief in God in practice is definitely right. My own belief in God is not forged in the practice of any individual religion, but in a general appreciation of the experience of the divine through many religious traditions and also in some ideas we'll get to soon (conversation three). But I do think it would be a mistake to think of God as a quasi-scientific hypothesis or as a mere thing among others. Moreover, I think that when we use terms of God like "goodness," "knowledge," or "purpose," we are (of course) using terms that we human beings have coined, and hence there is a danger that we can wind up wrongly projecting human features on that which transcends human reality.

PAT: Exactly. A danger I believe you have fallen into.

LIZ: Human terms are designed by us to describe and interact with the world as it is seen from our point of view. When you take human terms and then apply them to a supposedly transcendent reality, you are abusing language.

CHRIS: We shall see. I think we can use human language to refer to indefinitely many things that are nonhuman, from cats to galaxies. Let's discuss your charge in the next conversation. For now, though, let me register a worry. I do think there is also a danger of believing that "transcending logic" makes sense on any level: religiously, philosophically, morally, economically, or personally. If by "logic" we mean the laws of identity (A is A) and non-contradiction (A is not not-A) then, as I suggested earlier, we assert *nothing* when we flaunt these laws. If I say it is both true and not true that God is good, have I made any sense?

LIZ: You have made sense insofar as you find yourself refining and purifying a glimpse of God that can never be complete. For example, we can use the word "good" in different contexts. When I say "God is good," do I mean the same as "this book is good" or "look at the good race horse"? I would say that the term "good" means or designates different things depending upon the context. What makes a good race horse (it can run eighty kilometers per hour and be ridden effectively by a jockey) is not the same as what makes a good book. "Good" in these cases seems conditioned by the kind of thing at issue. But with God, there is no kind of thing—divinity—of which God happens to be the one. God is unique or, to say much the same thing, God is a unique reality making up its own kind (*sui generis*). The way to approach or address this supreme, transcendent reality cannot be through positive attributions, the so-called positive way or *via positiva*. It proves far better (or less futile) to engage in the negative way or the *via negativa*. So, for example, we can say that God is good but also beyond our notion of goodness; divine goodness is *not* like the created goodness of a book or the goodness of a horse or planet. God is beyond our best concepts.

CHRIS: I am deeply attracted to your position, though I resist it on the grounds that the negations you propose only make sense if there is some positive conception of God. That positive conception may be very patchy and incomplete, but doesn't there have to be some apprehension of what something *is* if we are to have some claim on knowing *what it is not*? Let me use a concrete example that emerged at the beginning of the dialogue. Pat questioned whether it makes any sense to think of God as a nonphysical, transcendent reality. I probably did not convince Pat that this is coherent, but in my view (for what it is worth) denying that God is a physical object—whether this is a chunk of matter or unit of energy—rests on some kind of positive conception of God as immaterial and spiritual, a being not subject to gravity or bounded by physical surfaces.

LIZ: But note that when you explain what you mean by immaterial—which is itself a negative term, that is, *not* material—you use negations. God is *not* subject to gravity or *not* bounded by a physical surface.

CHRIS: Good point. I do not dispel the use of negation at all. But I use negation on the basis of a positive concept of God as necessarily existing, all-knowing, all-powerful, all-good, omnipresent, and eternal or everlasting.

PAT: Okay, these may *seem* like positive attributes, but I think you have some work to do in spelling out what these attributes amount to.

CHRIS: On to the next conversation?

LIZ: By all means, and this is a conversation I welcome, but from a position that is slightly at odds with your project. I am interested in whether Chris can make a case for the coherence and plausibility of theism, but my final position is that even our very best concepts and arguments about the divine are all handicapped. God is beyond any human system of ideas or our best imagination and stories. I see the debate between theism and naturalism to be kind of like a debate over whether this figure is a duck or a rabbit:

It depends on how you look at it. Seen from one angle, it is a duck; seen from another, it is a rabbit. The debate is interesting: a duck is not a rabbit, and an atheist is not a theist. But I wish to point us to a God that is in some respects beyond both atheism and theism. The truth behind the duck-rabbit is an interwoven figure of black and white shapes, capable of being interpreted in two different ways. That is my view of the cosmos. One can see it theistically or atheistically, but the truth is beyond both.

QUESTIONS FOR FURTHER INQUIRY

1. Pat argues that the very idea of God does not make sense. What do you think the best methods are to determine whether an idea makes sense? Should the test include determining whether the idea is consistently describable? Or should it include determining whether one can imagine or picture or visually represent the object in dispute? How would you go about determining whether any of these other phenomena are possible: traveling backward in time; telekinesis; changing a frog's body into a human body; there being an event without a cause; or there being a first or last moment of time?

2. What is the best argument (in your view) for or against the coherence of there being a nonphysical, purposive, intentional agent?

3. Chris appeals to the necessity of the law of identity and necessary truths in mathematics for the coherence of God as a necessarily existing reality, whereas Pat sees necessity as merely a feature of language. Which view do you find more convincing? Is there a more promising view of the nature of necessity?

4. If the concept of God is a metaphysical impossibility, like a square circle, is it possible to believe that there is a God? If not, is the fact that many people believe there is a God some evidence that the concept of God is coherent?

NOTES

1. Michael Oakeshott, *The Voice of Poetry in the Conversation of Mankind* (London: Bowes and Bowes, 1959), 11.

2. Lewis Carroll, *Alice's Adventures in Wonderland* (Oxford: Oxford University Press, 1971), 9.

3. "Occam's razor," named after William of Occam (1290–1345), is the popular term for cutting away useless hypotheses. It has been formalized as "Entities should not be multiplied beyond necessity."

SECOND CONVERSATION

An Exploration of the Classical Understanding of God

> If there is no God, then God is incalculably the greatest
> single creation of the imagination. No other creature of
> [human beings'] imagination has been so fertile of ideas, so
> great an inspiration to philosophy, to literature, to painting,
> sculpture, architecture, and drama. Set beside the idea of
> God, the most original inventions of mathematicians and
> the most unforgettable characters in drama are minor prod-
> ucts of the imagination; Hamlet and the square root of mi-
> nus one pale into insignificance by comparison.
>
> —Anthony Kenny[1]

CHRIS: The concept of God in classical Judaism, Christianity, Islam, and in the theistic traditions in Hinduism, is that God is a spiritual or incorporeal reality, all-knowing (*omniscient*, from *omnis* meaning "all" and *scientia* or "knowledge"), all-powerful (*omnipotent*, from *omnis* meaning "all" and *potens* or "powerful"), all-good, omnipresent (there is no place where God is not), necessarily existing (God exists *a se*, or by God's own nature and not by virtue of any other power or reality), and eternal or everlasting. There are other attributes of God we might discuss, such as: divine impassability (the thesis that God does not have passions like joy, sorrow, love, anger), divine passability (the contrary thesis that God does have joy, sorrow, love, anger), and divine simplicity (God contains no parts). There are also ideas that God is worthy of worship and obedience, immutable (changeless), beautiful, holy (a quality of sacred otherness), and so on. Or we could look into specific accounts of the divine nature, such as the Christian belief that God is Triune and God became incarnate, but these can come into play in a later conversation. I accept a traditional form of theism, but I am currently undecided about accepting any specific theistic tradition.

PAT and LIZ together: Fair enough, let's go through the first set of divine attributes!

OMNISCIENCE

CHRIS: Alright—I have already spoken about God's necessary existence and incorporeality. I will try to make more headway on both God's necessity and incorporeality in the third conversation when I will argue that we have good reasons to think there is a nonphysical or incorporeal, necessarily existing, all-knowing, and good God, but for now I will explore the concepts of omniscience, being eternal or everlasting, omnipotence, goodness, and omnipresence. To say God is omniscient is to say that God knows all the truths that are possible to know.

PAT: A curious qualification about *possible* knowledge—before asking for clarification on that, I already see an objection. The very concept of "all knowledge" strikes me as puzzling. I can imagine all sorts of degrees of knowledge—you might know a person or thing better than I, and I can imagine someone having a greater scope of knowledge—you may know physics and chemistry whereas I only know chemistry. But *all knowledge* sounds like the concept of *a greatest possible number.* There cannot be such a thing. No matter how much an "omniscient" being knows, wouldn't there always be more?

CHRIS: Some cases of knowledge can be serialized or quantified numerically, but why see all cases of knowledge that way? Some philosophers think of God's cognition of all things in terms of unsurpassable perfection and precision; God's awareness is immediate. God does not have organs or a brain or a nervous system that must function reliably in order to secure accurate vision. Unlike us, God's awareness of visual and other properties does not require the photoreceptor protein rhodopsin. As for numbers, I think there would be a problem about omniscience if gaining complete knowledge required infinite stages of knowledge acquisition. So, if a being set out to learn the properties of each number (six is the successor of five; it is also the smallest perfect number—a number that is equal to the sum of its divisors including one, but not including itself, viz., 2 + 3 + 1 = 6; and it is also even, and so on) in a numerical series, it would never succeed. No matter how many numbers would be covered, there would be one more still. But one can know infinitely many truths in an instant or a moment: when I know you are under seven feet tall, I know you are under eight feet, under nine feet, under ten feet, and so on ad infinitum.

PAT: This appeal to immediate awareness troubles me. You seem to think it is an advantage to divine cognition that God does not have a brain or sense organs, but in proposing that God does not need such "equipment," aren't we in the same position as we were in during the first conversation about disembodiment? We simply have no clue what such cognition is like.

CHRIS: Unlike Liz, I think we can have a positive conception of unmediated awareness. Yes, as embodied beings we require brains, nervous systems, and more, but once I have a visual experience or tactile feeling I need not have some additional sense organ to see or feel. I am feeling warmth right now. I need all sorts of cognitive equipment and nerve endings to have the sensation and to realize the warmth is due to the sun's heat, but once I have the feeling, I have an *unmediated awareness of it*. This is what it means to have direct awareness, and this lack of mediation is befitting divine awareness.

PAT: Even if I grant you that, you are a long way from making sense of how God knows reality. Think further about immediate awareness: You may have immediate access to hot sensations and colors, but isn't this because they are states of your body? You feel hot because you *are* hot; you see red because your color field is red. If God has this immediate access to the cosmos, then isn't the cosmos part of God's body?

CHRIS: You may expect me to disagree completely with this suggestion, but I am prepared to think that while the cosmos is *not* God's body, there is a sense in which God has as direct or more direct access to the states of the cosmos as we have to our bodies. So, there is a sense in which God's relation to the cosmos is analogous to a person's relationship to her body. What prevents me from thinking the cosmos *is* God's body is that the cosmos has none of the other properties that make for a divine embodiment: the cosmos is not like a divine nervous system, brain, or skeleton, nor does the cosmos act as God's will, insofar as God has created free creatures who act against God's will.

PAT: We can return to the topic of whether God *could* take on or assume a material body (as I assume Christians believe about the incarnation), but I still have a central objection to the idea that an all-good God would be omniscient. It seems as though one needs to have certain experiences in order to know certain things. If I were blind, how could I know what seeing the color red is like? I might know that color experiences of red are derived from the spectral sensitivities of certain light receptors, but that is not the same thing as *knowing what red looks like*. If God is all-knowing, mustn't God know what red looks like? Mustn't God have to know what grapefruit juice tastes like? And mustn't an omniscient God even experience some suspect feelings like *knowing what it is like to be a serial killer or a pathological liar*? Some may think God only knows positive states of affairs, but once you think God must know everything, then it seems that God must undergo imperfect, even wicked states.

CHRIS: Well, even if God has to have sensations to know the relevant concepts, I don't see this as requiring moral defects. If a being felt that *it is wrong to feel like a serial killer or a pathological liar*, would that person be morally tarnished? I don't think so. The idea that God must know what it is like to feel some evil impulse does not imply any defect in God unless you are using the phrase "know what it's like" to mean *fully endorsing doing the relevant wicked acts*, or *endorsing the requisite emotions*. But I question the premise of your line of reasoning is that in order for a being to know some experiential concept of X, that being must experience X. Why? I do not need to be heavy to see that something is heavy, or to be cold to see that something is cold. I fully grant that seeing red is more than only knowing the physics of light and human anatomy (this is something I argued in the first conversation), but that is not the same thing as claiming that I need to experience red to know the concept of seeing red. Maybe given certain biological and neurological restraints, we do need such experiences, but it does not follow that all conceivable beings must be similarly limited.

PAT: I notice that in your line of reasoning you seem to appeal sometimes to what we can positively grasp (unmediated awareness) while at other times you seem to appeal to what we cannot rule out. So, in our last exchange you seem to have been challenging me to argue that a certain kind of cognition we lack is impossible for any being to have. Very well, let me work up an argument that does rule out omniscience.

FREEDOM AND FOREKNOWLEDGE

PAT continues: If a being is omniscient, it must know all truths, right? But then an omniscient being must know that it is true now that you will, for example, freely decide to go sailing tomorrow. But if it is true *now* that you will go sailing *tomorrow*, how could you not go sailing? Freedom, it seems, involves the power to do otherwise! You freely do X (whatever), so long as you do X but could have not done X. This is sometimes called *libertarian freedom* or incompatiblism, because it asserts that when a free agent does something she is not compelled to do the act by external forces, antecedent conditions, or the laws of nature. In other words, libertarian freedom is incompatible with a fully determined cosmos. (Defenders of libertarian freedom like to point out that contemporary science allows that there is a genuine indeterminism in the cosmos, at least at the quantum level.) I present you with the following dilemma: if God knows your supposedly free future action, then that action is not actually free because you could not do other than what God knows you will do. Alternatively, if God does not know your future free action, then God is not omniscient. I conclude that either you lack freedom (at least you lack libertarian freedom), or God is not omniscient.

CHRIS: This is a powerful argument, and I confess that I have not decided which solution to adopt. Currently, I affirm the reality of future free action and take the position that most philosophers attribute to Aristotle: future free action is undetermined. To put this option succinctly: it is neither true nor false now whether or not I will freely sail tomorrow. There is not yet a fact of the matter that makes it true or false, and there will not be a truth about what I will do until the time occurs. In my view, omniscience involves *knowing all the truths it is possible to know*. But if future free action is neither true nor false, an omniscient being need not (and cannot) know future, free, contingent states of affairs.

PAT: I find this a very radical move on your part. Doesn't it seem rather that it is true now that you will do such and such in the future? Maybe you and I cannot know it, but don't we *discover* the truth tomorrow?

CHRIS: That is a natural way to put things, but I think it is also misleading. We often work with a spatial model of time in which the future is in front of us and the past is behind us. Or we think of time like a river. But does this imagery really hold up? I am instead of the mind that the future does not exist out there in front of us, like a land we come to discover. The future, unlike the past, is something that we can (in part) create. It is up to you now what your future will be like.

PAT: You know, there is an alternative I thought you might take, which is that freedom does not involve the ability to do otherwise. Let's discuss this option when we address the problem of evil. For now, let me simply point out that you are working with a concept that is severely limited from the standpoint of the classical religions you started from. Don't the Hebrew Bible, the Christian New Testament, and the Qur'an portray God as knowing the future? I thought this was a part of the whole concept of a prophet who proclaims future free action. Don't prophets foretell the future in light of God's alleged perfect knowledge of the future?

CHRIS: Actually, the role of prophecy in these traditions is often focused on the immediate circumstances facing the followers of God. A prophet might expose what he or she decrees as the moral debasement of their community. But as for future prophetic visions, these seem (perhaps surprisingly) open-ended. In *Jonah*, for example, there is a prophetic proclamation about the imminent destruction of the city of Nineveh. But the narrative goes on: disaster is averted because the people repent. A prophecy may signal a divine intention or purpose and yet its consequences can still be contingent upon future free action.

PAT: This still seems to be quite a shift from the traditional concept of God. And while some traditional prophecy may be open-ended, a great deal of the early case for Christianity involved the claim that the coming of the Messiah was foreseen. But my deeper worry isn't so much biblical consistency as it is whether you are defending a very diminished form of theism. For example, in your view, could God be surprised by future free action?

CHRIS: Not like us. If this qualified account of omniscience is right, God knows all possible futures; God knows the present and past inexhaustibly and unsurpassably. From this vantage point, you cannot surprise an omniscient being by some unpredictable action or, to adopt an absurd example, coming up with a joke with an ending that God has not thought about. But while I am satisfied with this analysis of omniscience, I am not prepared to rule out the idea that God is eternal, transcending all time. This more encompassing position would provide grounds for prophetic foreknowledge, whereas on my account things like Messianic prophesies will have to be comparatively open-ended (expressing divine intentions but not strictly fixing the future). On the open-ended account, the foretold incarnation might not have occurred if, for example, Mary said "no." But if we adopt the view that God transcends time, Mary's free consent to the incarnation might be known timelessly. Let me take this idea one step further:

Some thinkers conceive of the cosmos in terms of an infinite set of alternate realities, in which the realization of each possible action or event spawns another reality. So if I decide to go sailing tomorrow, that is one reality, while if I decide to stay home and read, that is a different, but parallel, reality. I think it is possible for God to conceive of all possible realities at once—those of the past, present, and future. Additionally, since I maintain that God is omniscient, God must be able to know not only of every possible reality, but also know which realities have actually occurred, are occurring, and may occur. Of those that may occur, perhaps God knows some which will necessarily occur—significant events in the history of the universe—but that leaves most decisions we make on a daily basis still undetermined and not known by God.

PAT: That is an interesting idea, but I don't think it succeeds in truly solving the problem of God's omniscience and free will. It seems to me that you are hedging on each side of the debate in order to come to a conclusion that helps God escape the contradiction of omniscience versus free will. You have put forward an interesting framework, but it is one that ultimately disregards the logical incongruity of God knowing *everything* while still not being sure. Either God knows what will happen in the future or not, and if God does know the future, then it is no longer for us to freely decide. It seems to me that you have tried to alter the definition of omniscience, and that you place arbitrary levels of importance on cosmic events.

CHRIS: Ouch! I concede the point that if future free action is incompatible with foreknowledge, then it is implausible to believe God foreknows only *some* free action. But I do *not* think it is arbitrary to claim that being omniscient should cover only *possible* knowledge, and if knowing future free action is *impossible*, then there is no reason to think that God or some other omniscient being has such knowledge.

ETERNAL OR EVERLASTING OMNISCIENCE

CHRIS continues: I cannot at this point embrace the view that God transcends time, because I believe it winds up treating the future as though it (in some sense) exists now or at least exists now before God's all-embracing omniscient life. If God from eternity knows I would freely go sailing tomorrow, I suspect I could not do otherwise. But the notion that God is eternal is a deep one historically; it was embraced by Augustine, Boetheus, and Aquinas, and it is defended by a host of philosophers today like Brian Leflow and Eleonore Stump. Boethius (sixth century) famously described God's life as an ideal completeness beyond change. "Eternity . . . is the complete simultaneous and perfect possession of everlasting life . . . and if human and divine present can be compared, just as you see certain things in this your present time, so God sees all things in this eternal present."[2]

PAT: All this might be relevant for our dialogue about evil. To what extent, in creating the cosmos, did God know about the magnitude of suffering?

CHRIS: That is a fair enough question to take up later. My current preferred view is that God is everlasting (without temporal beginning or end) rather than eternal, but let's revisit this later.

PAT: I am still not happy with your analysis of omniscience. Given that your preferred treatment of God and time is that God is temporal, then I assume your view of omniscience needs to be indexed to time. That is, you will need to hold that a being (or God) is omniscient at a given time (which we could symbolize as t) if that being knows all the truths it is possible to know at t. But at t_2 and t_3 there will be more to know, so your omniscient being would not so much have supreme or absolute knowledge; it would be learning more each day! I persist in thinking you are adopting a position that is a bit too anthropomorphic and at odds with the traditions you claim to defend.

CHRIS: There is a sense in which I think this is quite right about God coming to know more over time, but I don't see this as a diminishing of the divine. I actually think an omniscient being would have to grow continuously in cognition or shift in awareness, knowing *now* that it is Wednesday, two p.m., Central Standard Time, here in North America, and knowing *now* it is two p.m. and three seconds, and *now* another two seconds have elapsed. Insofar as time involves real change, there would have to be real change in the scope of omniscience. The view of God I am commending may be considered *existentialist* (existentialist philosophers in the twentieth century gave primary emphasis on the reality of the present movement) and it is sometimes called *presentism* (only the present exists).

PAT: I thought contemporary physics has taught us there is no absolute "now" and that temporality is relative to a frame of reference.

CHRIS: Some of my friends appeal to contemporary physics to bolster the classical thesis that God transcends time, but I am more comfortable philosophically with thinking that God is everlasting, without temporal beginning or end. I have my doubts about the denial of an absolute now.

If there is no absolute "now," then my view is that God's frame of reference is maximal, insofar as it encompasses all other possible "nows" or frames of reference.

PAT: In your view, God did not create time.

CHRIS: Right; but I do not thereby see God as less excellent or somehow subject to "time" as God's ruler or master. The existence of time consists of there being a past, present, and future. For us, time might seem corrosive because of our diminished powers in old age, our fading memories, and so on. But if God is non-contingent, omnipotent, omniscient, all-good, and so on, then God is not at all subject to corrosion, degeneration, or weakening powers. On the view that God is everlasting, it would make no sense to think of God as old; it would make better sense to describe God as ageless. I also find it more difficult to think of the God of traditional theism as transcending all temporality.

PAT: As an atheist, I find both the notions that God is eternal and that God is simply everlasting equally muddled, but I can't resist taking note of the instability of your concept of God. On the one hand you appeal to religious texts that describe God as the Creator of all. Intuitively, I would say "all" would have to include both space and time. But then it seems that you start hedging the traditional view once you believe it threatens future free action. How do you make decisions about what you believe? Why not stick to the tradition that God transcends and created time and jettison the belief in libertarian freedom? Isn't this a bit like playing tennis without a net or any rules whatsoever?

CHRIS: For reasons that I sketched earlier, I take as my central thesis that our core theistic concept of God—as forged by religious experience and tradition—is the concept of a being of great excellence. This tenet was formalized by St. Anselm (1033–1109) as the thesis that God is that which none greater can be conceived. In other words, God is unsurpassably great or maximally excellent. While it may appear that being eternal or beyond time is a supreme excellence, I think further reflection should lead us to affirm God is temporal. This is not just because if God is eternal, then God cannot create a cosmos where there is genuine freedom; I also think if God is eternal, God would not be a personal or person-like reality. If God is eternal, God would be changeless, and I cannot imagine a changeless person or personal reality. So my denying of God's eternality is not a capricious move in an un-tennis game. I affirm God's being everlasting rather than eternal as the former is entailed by maximal excellence. An eternal God would lack an excellence possessed by an everlasting God.

PAT: Why should being a person be thought of as supremely excellent or unsurpassably great? Why not posit some abstract great property, like justice, or some sublime state of the cosmos? Being a person seems very terrestrial and limiting.

CHRIS: Being a person may be terrestrial and limiting if we only focus on humans, but the way I propose using the term *person* (or *personal reality*) is that it refers to a subject that is conscious and possesses cognitive awareness and powers of free agency (is capable of acting intentionally). Some persons have these properties in highly limited cases (human infants, and perhaps some nonhuman animals, such as porpoises and dolphins, are persons), but I submit we can imagine these powers at superlative levels—in theism. I believe these powers are true, great-making excellences. Imagine any excellence—a stunning sun or galaxy or body of matter or vast energy—what would be more excellent? A being that could choose to knowingly create and conserve these and much more in existence, and to have that level of power, would require the excellence that I suggest constitutes being a person.

PAT: Be careful how many of these convictions may haunt you later. If God is so excellent, why is there evil? This will be the heart of our fourth conversation.

OMNIPOTENCE AND GOODNESS

PAT continues: If we are now on to omnipotence, I have two objections. The first may appear to be a mere word game and of little interest, but the second is deeper. First the teaser: if God is all-powerful, God can do anything. If God can do anything, then God can create a stone too heavy for any being to lift. If there were a stone too heavy for any being to lift, God could not lift it. Hence God is not omnipotent; for either God cannot make a stone too heavy for any being to lift, or God cannot lift a stone too heavy for any being to lift.

CHRIS: Power is not measured by the ability to do what is logically contradictory; the very concept of the stone in question is a logical contradiction. There cannot be a stone so heavy that it cannot be lifted by a being that can lift any stone whatsoever. This "teaser" objection to omnipotence is, indeed, a mere teaser, for it can be multiplied without end: could God eat porridge that is uneatable? Or ride a bike that cannot be ridden? Or can God do what God cannot do? None of these involve limitations of divine power. These puzzles emerge as the result of an explicit built-in contradiction which creates nonsense, such as the idea that there could be a triangle without three sides.

PAT: I am willing to grant that, but get ready for a more serious challenge. You believe God is essentially good, yes? What does that mean?

CHRIS: It means that God can do no evil.

PAT: Well, then, it seems that I am more powerful than God, for I can do all sorts of things (lie, cheat, and steal, for instance) that God cannot do. Moreover, it appears that there can be a being more powerful than God, as you conceive God. Imagine two beings, Yahweh and Melkor; both have equal power, except that Yahweh can only do good acts, whereas Melkor can do either good or evil acts. Isn't Melkor more powerful than Yahweh?

CHRIS: It is an argument like that which prompts some theists to claim that while God is good, God is not essentially or necessarily good. That is, while God can do evil, God does not. This option also allows some theists a straightforward treatment of God being worthy of praise. In my view, God *cannot* do evil, but in the alternative view of God, God can be praised for doing good.

PAT: So you don't think God is worthy of praise?

CHRIS: I do. Praise is central to my understanding of God. In fact—as I suggested earlier in discussing divine excellence—I believe what drives the classical understanding of God is praise or, more broadly, awe and adoration. So while the Hebrew Bible, Christian New Testament, and Qur'an offer a variety of portraits of God, each also depicts God as worthy of our highest praise. The Qur'an for example, begins on its first page with praise to Allah. Praise may be given to us for doing good when we might have done evil, but I think praise (wonder, awe, delight) is due to God for God's essential goodness. This is a delight in the divine nature itself as well as awe that God does good when it is not strictly necessitated. This is not a form of moral praise (which strikes me as somewhat misplaced when it comes to God—as if we are expressing gratitude and relief that God is well behaved) but of a higher praise in the sheer essential goodness of God. As for comparing a God of essential goodness to a being who could do good or evil, does Melkor have an excellence that Yahweh lacks? I suggest the answer is no. The so-called power to do evil is not an actual power but a corrosive deficiency. The "power" to murder and rape is not a power that is worthy of worship or praise or a great-making excellence. In attributing power to God, religious theists are not exalting what might be called bare, naked, or brutal power, but a kind of holy, excellent power. So, in my view God is to be praised because of God's essential goodness (we are to take awesome delight in God's good power), but this is different from praising God for doing good when, if God were to turn to evil, God would be your enemy.

PAT: I suggest your depiction of God is not at all consistent with the scriptural traditions to which you appeal. Don't get me wrong. I have no desire myself to praise either Melkor or Yahweh. It's just that you seem to be crafting a concept of God that is out of step with the religions you seem to believe are live options. The God of the Bible seems quite wild. God seems to countenance and even insist on the death penalty for minor infractions (Leviticus 21:9). God seems to have commanded the slaughter of whole cities and peoples (Deuteronomy 20:16–17; Joshua 6:20–21), God seems to ban homosexuality (Leviticus 20:13, Romans 1:26–27). God is also described as jealous (Exodus 20:5). How do you square all this with the concept of God being an essentially good or maximally excellent being?

CHRIS: Well, I am not, at least not yet, a Christian or a member of any religious tradition, but let me sketch a reply. One could treat these scriptural accounts as literally true and then argue that under those conditions the divine precepts were binding. Some argue that the ban on homosexuality was historically prompted by a prohibition against homosexual temple prostitutes, and would not be binding on an alternative healthy case of consensual same-sex union. Or, with respect to a divinely sanctioned killing of whole city populations, someone might argue that this was warranted because of profound, embedded evils of the people. For example, it has been argued that those whom God commanded Joshua to kill were committed to child sacrifice and other evils. It is possible to read the story of God destroying the cities of Sodom and Gomorrah as a condemnation of rape. I am an outsider to this debate; however, if I were to subscribe to a biblical tradition, I would adopt the view that revelation of God is genuine but mediated by imperfect human sources. I would probably treat the story of God destroying all creation with a great flood yet saving Noah as a narrative designed to instruct us that we should shun wickedness; our evil can bring about a destruction of nature; and we should rescue as many natural goods (animals) as possible. In other words, it is possible to treat biblical narratives in more ways than either literal history or pure mythology. If there is an essentially good God, why should one expect that God would reveal the nature of moral perfection to us from the beginning of human development any more than God would reveal the deep truths of physics we are only now discovering? Theists might claim that the God depicted in the Bible is an exact, precise portrait, reliable in all details, but theists may also claim that God is to be found *through* the Bible, which is a record of the gradual, progressive revelation of God. My current view is that God is revealed in multiple scriptures, from Christian scripture to the Hindu Bhagavad Gita. As for God being portrayed as jealous, I do not have a problem with such an attribution so long as God is understood under the category of essential goodness. Imagine there is an essentially good Creator God and creatures relentlessly afflict each other with cruelty. The jealousy of God might consist in God's sorrow (or perhaps even anger) when people injure rather than help each other.

PAT: This is not really the point of divine jealousy in the Hebrew Bible or Christian Old Testament. The biblical God does not want the chosen people to worship other gods. The biblical God is like a jilted, jealous husband, or an angry parent upset that his child seeks a different father.

CHRIS: Fair point. I still do not see a problem, though. If God is essentially good, and living in concord with God is good, then God's jealousy can be understood as God's fitting sorrow and anger that God's people are renouncing goodness in favor of destruction. Imagine a parent-child relationship that is healthy until the child goes to college and falls in love with a corrupt, drug-taking, alcoholic, pornography-using philosophy professor whom the child idealizes as her or his new father. If the real father felt sorrow and anger, wouldn't this be fitting? We might even think the parent wasn't really loving if the parent had no such emotions.

PAT: Your position still seems innately unstable and dangerous morally, even religiously. Isn't the religious practitioner supposed to be led by God? In your view, scripture cannot really be something that guides "the believer," unless scripture already agrees with what the believer thinks is God and what the believer thinks is good. This seems to be a case of the believer judging God rather than vice versa. But if you don't take that route, scripture seems to justify all kinds of aberrations, including slavery (Leviticus 25:44–46).

CHRIS: I don't yet see a problem that we can avoid irrespective of whether you believe in God or not. I assume you grant that we human beings have slowly achieved greater wisdom and moral insight over time. At one point, few believed slavery was wrong. Similarly, there have been times when people mistakenly thought God approved of slavery when this was not the case. Our views of both morality and God develop progressively.

PAT: But look, for those who think there is a God, they think that they might have a direct access to some profound moral truths that none of the rest of us can have. That is simply dangerous.

CHRIS: There can be dangers but also opportunities. Consider the case of Martin Luther King Jr. and others who fought against racism in North America in the nineteenth and twentieth centuries. Many of them did so out of an overt belief that they were responding to the experience of a just, provident God. And look at the stability offered in traditional religion and the way religious reasoning accords with secular moral reasoning. I shall argue that there are stabilizing factors in both secular ethics and in thinking about ethics from a God's eye point of view.

GOODNESS, SECULAR AND RELIGIOUS REFLECTIONS ON VALUES

CHRIS continues: When you are making a moral decision about sexual ethics, abortion, suicide, war, or any other topic, don't you try to know as much as possible about all the facts that form the basis of your moral judgment? If you are wondering whether it is permissible to go to war with another nation, don't you want to get as clear a view as possible about whether the nation has actually attacked you or is genuinely on the verge of such an attack? If it is threatening you, why is it doing so? Perhaps what you initially saw as baseless aggression is actually an honest, well-intentioned response to something your nation has done recklessly. After getting clear about all such facts, then moral reasoning seems to involve an appeal to emotions. Do you affectively know what it is like to go to war? Perhaps you have never seen or experienced violence. It seems natural in an argument about war that we challenge each other to think deeply and profoundly about the points of view (and the lives!) of all involved parties. This seems to me to be fundamentally practicing the Golden Rule of weighing whether you should do unto others as you would have them do to you. In order to use this precept you really do need to put yourself in another person's position. An additional feature of moral reasoning is *impartiality*—in merely thinking about only what I will get out of some action, I am being biased and partial; mature moral reflection must include striving for impartiality. To summarize: moral reflection involves striving for a comprehensive understanding of all the facts on which to base one's moral judgment; it involves being affectively aware of the points of view of all parties; and it involves impartiality. If I am right about these three ideals, then I suggest that ideal moral reasoning involves seeking a God's eye point of view.

PAT: Let me see if I understand you. I am an atheist. Are you claiming that when I think ethically I am striving for the point of view of a being that I think does not exist?

CHRIS: Not exactly. Certainly you are not overtly and consciously striving to get a view that you think would be had by a merely hypothetical or nonexistent observer. But note the ideals you are using in moral reflection: complete knowledge of the facts on the basis of which you will make a moral judgment, affective awareness of all involved parties, and impartiality. These are all ideals that make up a God's eye point of view—if there is a God.

PAT: But when I engage in ethical reflection, I am not seeking omniscience, Chris! I am seeking enough relevant knowledge to make the right decision.

CHRIS: Okay, but isn't the very concept of *relevant knowledge* something that is definable in terms of a kind of omniscience: *one knows the relevant facts when there is no additional knowledge needed* or *one knows that no more knowledge will alter one's judgment.*

PAT: I think you are pressing your point too far. As a marathon runner, I try to do my best in a race but I do not aim at some ideal like a constant sprint from starting point to finish line. My deeper objection, though, is that the theistic God does not seem like a great candidate for your ideal observer. The God I see in various scriptures, *for example,* seems exceedingly partial and not especially sensitive to the affective points of view of all parties. Earlier I brought up the case of scriptures portraying God as jealous. That is not all. God seems exceedingly vain and envious. It appears that the God of your theistic traditions wants worship and gets quite angry if you do not do what God wants. I might admire your effort to bring religious reasoning into some accord with my secular moral reasoning, but you still are weighed down by a distracting supernaturalism. Why look to God for directions, when you can simply seek knowledge, affective awareness, and impartiality on your own? We can strive for comprehensive knowledge, impartiality, and affective clarity without invoking some supernatural, distracting reference point.

CHRIS: I have three replies. First, the God of the great monotheistic religions is portrayed as acting in particular ways (e.g., guiding "the chosen people"), but in each tradition, the sustained teaching is that any such particular action is for the good (ultimately) of all creation. More-over, each of these traditions has been pitted against partiality and un-fairness (e.g., James 1). Second, if you believe God is essentially good, praising God is not praising an ego; it is more like feeling awe or plea-sure and delight in essential goodness itself. This reply goes back to my previous response about jealousy; vanity, jealousy, and envy are all vices if we think of them as cruel ways in which someone dishonorably as-sumes they possess another person. But again, if God is essential good-ness, matters shift. Third, I suggest the appeal to a God's eye point of view is not as remote as you think. To test this, consider the following thought experiment: advance any position on any ethical topic you like that you are convinced about. Is it coherent for you to claim that you believe X (whatever it is) is morally permissible and yet you also believe that if you knew more facts, if you were more affectively aware of the points of views of others and you weren't biased, you would believe X is wrong? I propose that such a claim would be self-defeating or inco-herent. Imagine claiming you think the current use of nuclear power is morally permissible but you would reverse this judgment if you actually knew the physics involved. Your judgment that such an energy policy is wrong is (presumably) based on what you believe is accurate physics and not what you know would be overturned given further inquiry.

PAT: I don't think this appeal to a God's eye point of view is very useful, in part because I see no reason to think that there is a God.

CHRIS: Though, if it turns out that both religious and secular reasoning about values are similar in terms of seeking impartiality, affective ap-praisal, and the widest scope of knowledge, this would show us to be on the same side, so to speak.

PAT: In theory, yes, but in practice I still worry about allowing any ap-peal to God whatsoever. Only too often, one finds a religious group that believes God has given them a promised land that another group denies. You have been trying to show that theists employ a method of deter-mining what is good that is similar to my secular, nonreligious moral re-flection. But this leaves out a crucial dimension of so much religious, theistic tradition. You seem to be arguing or assuming that God disapproves of slavery because slavery is wrong (even if it took a while, on your account, for us to realize God condemns slavery). And yet it seems that most religious theists would put far more central emphasis on God's commands, according to which slavery is wrong because God condemns it. Therein lies my problem with traditional theism. I cannot believe that slavery, rape, and murder, among other deeds, are wrong, or that compassion is good, simply because of God's commands. To make ethics depend on God is to undermine ethics. What if God commanded that we routinely execute innocent people for the sake of entertainment? Would that then become morally right?

CHRIS: You often warn me that I am adjusting my version of theism to distance myself from theistic, religious traditions. But keep in mind that in many revealed, sacred texts it seems that God delights in what is good (Genesis 1: after each creation, we read "And God saw that it was good"). This suggests that there is something valuable that God delights in, rather than a matter of something (the earth, say) being good because of God's delight. In my view, God cannot command something evil for its own sake, such as homicide for the sake of entertainment.

PAT: There is, however, a biblical story in which God commands a father, Abraham, to sacrifice his son Isaac—a completely innocent child. The sacrifice is prevented at the last possible moment by divine revelation, and yet the fact that there was a wicked command to begin with is a problem.

CHRIS: Probably the easiest way to handle this narrative that appears in Genesis, chapter 21, is to see it as affirming that the God of the Hebrews does *not* require such a sacrifice. The role of the story is to press home the view that while God may appear to be like the other gods (assuming the surrounding Canaanites' gods called for sacrifices of children), God is *not* like them.

PAT: But surely you must see that if values or goodness are independent of God's will, God is subordinate to something greater than God. And yet surely this exposes a problem, for God is supposed to be a sovereign of the highest possible authority.

CHRIS: Some theists claim that all valuations do stem from God's will. They embrace what is called the divine command theory, according to which what makes things good is that God commands them. I accept a somewhat middle ground: I suggest that God's very nature is essentially good; goodness is thus not something above God or sovereign over God's will. Because goodness is a part of God's very nature, God cannot arbitrarily reverse the divine nature and make cruelty good and compassion evil. Still, I think that God's will can make some things obligatory that would not be so otherwise. Imagine you are considering two states of affairs that are equally good—going to medical school or business school—but you have reason to believe that God calls you to medical school. Perhaps this reason stems from religious experience, or maybe your study of sacred texts leads you to believe God subordinates economic values to health and you are living in a community where there are many merchants but few physicians. This background might well lead you to believe that, if there is a God, God calls one to pursue a vocation in medicine. However you reach such a conclusion, I suggest that if there is an essentially good God and God wills that you pursue one good rather than another, the divinely willed good becomes not merely permissable, but obligatory.

PAT: Well, your position may appear to be less subject to divine whim, but you are still letting "God" operate as a dangerous moral force. What if you are neutral about capital punishment, but you believe God has a special interest in executing people?

CHRIS: Well, that is a danger, but the traditionally theistic religions have all given the greatest testimony to God being compassionate and merciful, rather than vengeful.

PAT: What I am still missing from your account is *why* God's commands should matter at all. Is it because God backs up commands with threats? Appeal to brute power will not generate obligations. If someone comes up to you with a gun and demands your money or he or she will kill you, it may be that you are obliged to give the money in the sense that it is prudent or in your interest to do so. But that does not mean you have an ethical duty to surrender the money.

CHRIS: I agree completely. Material or emotional threats alone do not generate obligations to help thieves. The root of divine authority, in my view, stems from divine creation and the value of a relationship between God and creatures. Since we are created by God, we owe God a debt of gratitude for our creation and conservation, and as for relationships, I believe that there is great good in being in concord with a loving, essentially good Creator. This is borne out in the value of religious experience.

PAT: As you know, I challenge both the goodness of the cosmos as well as the credibility of religious experience.

CHRIS: Yes, and I will try to defend both in the following conversations.

PAT: Let's move on to get the key arguments as to why you think there actually is a God, making good on your promise to justify your beliefs about God accounting for the cosmos, religious experience, and so on.

CHRIS: Absolutely. In the next conversation I will develop four arguments for God's existence, and in the fourth conversation let's focus on the problem of evil. But before doing so, let me quickly fill out two other divine attributes—divine omnipresence and passability—and then check in with Liz.

OMNIPRESENCE AND PASSABILITY

CHRIS continues: In believing that God is omnipresent, one believes there is no place God is not. As God is nonphysical or spiritual, God's presence is not like the presence of any matter or energy, but a function of God's creativity, power, and knowledge. So to say that God is *here*, for example, means that this place (like all other places) would not exist without God's active sustaining of this place in existence, God can exercise power here (creating or destroying or moving whatever), and God has unsurpassable awareness of all that occurs here. God's passability is God's affective responsiveness to values: God sorrows over ill and evil, and God takes pleasure in good. Some theologians and philosophers adopt, instead, a form of impassabilism, according to which God has no sorrow or pleasure. Liz, I imagine, holds a form of impassabilism.

LIZ: In a sense, yes. I think terms like "sorrow" and "pleasure" make sense in relationship to human and nonhuman animal life, but not to the unique God beyond all such spatiotemporal categories. I enjoyed the exchange between you, though I believe that whatever the outcome, the end goal is not achievable by reason or human categories. The pathway to the divine is even *against* reason. By using reason alone, I cannot imagine God or Melkor creating ex nihilo (from nothing). All creation we observe involves material exchange or putting together sensations or ideas built on our experience. I am rather inclined to think creation from nothing is logically absurd. But faith in God is not a matter of logic or images.

INEFFABILITY

PAT: I am very critical of Chris's *via positive*, but your way of negation, Liz, puzzles me deeply. You earlier spoke about addressing but not describing God. But in order to address God, don't you have to have some positive understanding of God? Imagine I tell you I love something (X) but I have absolutely no positive conception of X. I don't see how it is possible to have any emotions about something without some picture or image of that thing. And getting the right image is crucial. For example, imagine I claim to love Chris because she or he is (I think) a firefighter-novelist-physician who won a Nobel Peace Prize but it turns out I am wrong and Chris is an arsonist, book-burning faith-healer who hates peace. I would say in this case I did not really love Chris, but an image of Chris. Now in the case of Chris the theist—because I think there is no God—I believe that Chris is not actually worshipping or loving God, but rather a mere image of God. In your case, Liz, when you have no image of God whatsoever, I think you not only do not or cannot worship or praise or love God, you cannot even worship an image; instead you are addressing something that seems like nothing.

LIZ: This last point may be intended to be an objection, but I rather like your line of reasoning. To ordinary perception and experience, God may appear to be nothing, but this is because God is beyond *everything*. God is ineffable or incapable of being described, at least of *literal* description (we can use some metaphors and analogies), because God is beyond the domain of this cosmos. Our language works fine for things in this world, but moving beyond this world requires a shift in meaning and personal orientation. While the next conversation may focus on you and Chris, I will slip in an argument of my own near the end to take seriously the *via negativa*.

THEISM AND NATURALISM

PAT: Good. But as we turn to weigh Chris's arguments, it may prove useful to summarize the differences between us. I am solidly grounded in the natural sciences. When we want to explain some phenomenon like biological inheritance, we may begin by positing something we do not know in detail (a gene) but then we go on to learn about DNA and RNA. Our explanation becomes richer as we see how different chemical and biological processes function. In the case of God, however, I am at a loss. In a sense, I agree with Liz that I can form no logical portrait of God creating ex nihilo or doing or knowing anything. The idea that one could explain anything by an appeal to an incorporeal, powerful, good agent strikes me as preposterous. In Genesis, explanations seem to proceed by appeal to God, saying "let there be light." This kind of explanation seems to be a case of magic.

CHRIS: Forcefully stated! The kind of explanation you find in Genesis is called *teleological* and *intentional*. It involves an appeal to purposes and reasons, and it is a fundamental and—I suggest—irreducible and fully respectable mode of explanation in all human experience. The kinds of explanations about deoxyribonucleic acid, or DNA, that you appeal to involve causes but not reasons. These kinds of explanations are fine so long as we put to one side human psychology, motives, reasoning, and purposive intentions. But once the latter comes into the picture, we can appeal to good or bad reasons, well-thought-out or unsuccessful plans, wise or foolish ideas. Contrary to you and Liz, I think we can very ably conceive of events being brought about intentionally because this happens during virtually every waking moment. As for creating ex nihilo, we seem to be able to appreciate how great artists compose new symphonies or create worlds of fiction, and so on.

PAT: But all such creation relies on prior ideas artists get from the world.

CHRIS: Many theists such as myself hold that God's omniscience covers all conceivable, possible states of affairs. We do not see the creation of the cosmos as God literally saying "let there be light" in some vague sort of way and then, zap, we get some electromagnetic radiation, or, using big bang cosmology, 14 to 15 billion years ago God said "let there be dust and gas." All conceivable forms of dust, gas, radiation, cells, quarks, leptons, and so on are all (if there is an omniscient God) in the mind of God. Creation consists of God bringing about states of affairs that God fully grasps with unsurpassable exactitude (in a phrase: cognition or knowledge precedes, or is antecedent to, volition or creation). This mode of explanation is on a magnitude surpassing our detailed imagination, but it is a basic form of explanation we appeal to every day involving goals and values. Imagine you want to read a book called *Dialogues about God* in a room that is dark. You might call out to me "Let there be light!" and I would light a candle. Why did you call out? There may be lots of causes, but if your request was an act that you did intentionally, it must in some sense be *basic* and explained in terms of reasons (you want to read a dialogue to stimulate your own thinking about God) and not explained away or reduced to other non-intentional causes. Intentional, basic explanations are not magic. My thesis in our next conversation is that a divine teleological explanation of the cosmos is able to make sense of why the cosmos is a coherent causal network, and why your science is successful.

PAT and LIZ: Let's move ahead.

QUESTIONS FOR FURTHER INQUIRY

1. Can an omniscient being be essentially good?
2. If God knows all states of the cosmos in an unmediated, direct way, is the cosmos analogous to God's body? If so, is that a problem?

3. If God is omniscient, can God know future free action? Why or why not?

4. Can an omnipresent being be essentially good?

5. Could there be an eternal God who transcends time?

6. In articulating the concept that God is good, Chris employs what is called an ideal observer theory of ethics. Essentially the idea is that sound moral reflection involves pursuing a maximum comprehensive knowledge, affective awareness, and impartiality, the point of view of an ideal judge or observer. Chris then links this with a God's eye point of view. What are the best reasons for and against an ideal observer theory?

7. Pat questions whether Chris is remaining faithful to the religious concepts of God that Chris seeks to defend. Pat is here expressing a distinction that Pascal (1623–1662) posed between the God of religion and the God of philosophy. Chris seeks to employ the method derived from Anselm that gives primacy to the idea that God is maximally excellent, e.g., if the God of a religion appears less than maximally excellent, this is a mere appearance and not a literally true or precisely accurate understanding of God. What are the merits or demerits of this Anselmian method?

8. If God transcends all human images and language, can God be loved or praised? Why or why not?

NOTES

1. Anthony Kenny, *Faith and Philosophy* (New York: Colombia University Press, 1983), 59.

2. Boethius, *The Consolation of Philosophy*, Book V, Prose 6, trans. V. E. Watts (London: Penguin Books, 1969), 163, 165–66.

THIRD CONVERSATION

Arguments for the Existence of God

"My mind," he said, "rebels at stagnation. Give me problems, give me work, give me . . . the most intricate analysis, and I am in my proper atmosphere. I can dispense then with artificial stimulants."

—Sherlock Holmes in "The Science of Deduction"[1]

CHRIS: I will advance four arguments for God's existence against Pat's secular naturalism. One may be called an *ontological argument*, and the others a *cosmological argument*, a rather comprehensive *teleological argument*, and finally an *argument from religious experience*.

PAT and LIZ: Any time you are ready, but one at a time, please!

AN ONTOLOGICAL ARGUMENT

CHRIS: This first argument is notorious for its abstract formulation and it has had few advocates, but it has also attracted massive attention and I find it convincing. Even if it does not convince you, however, it is useful in highlighting my central claim in our first conversation that the concept of God is the concept of a necessarily existing being.

PAT and LIZ: Carry on!

CHRIS: Very well. Consider four different terms that are described as *modal*, in that they refer to the mode of states of affairs: necessary, impossible, possible, and contingent. Examples of each include: $1 + 1 = 2$ is necessary; a round square is impossible; you and I are possible; and *there is a cat in a tree* is contingent. Each of these modal terms is inter-definable, so consider the following translations: *$1 + 1 = 2$ is necessary* equals *$1 + 1$ is not equal to 2 is impossible*. Or: *$1 + 1 = 2$ is possible* is equivalent to *$1 + 1 \neq 2$ is impossible*. *A round square is impossible* is equivalent to: *it is necessary that there can be no round square*. Or: *it is contingent that the cat is in the tree* is equivalent to: *it is possible that the cat is in a tree and it is possible that the cat is not in the tree*. I know this may seem a tad abstruse, but let me bring to light how these modal relations come to bear on the question of God's existence. I will develop an ontological argument in four steps.

Premise One: If God exists, God exists necessarily. This is, I believe, not some arbitrary definition but a reflection of how God is conceived in religious tradition. It may also be supported by the appeal to divine excellence developed in our earlier conversations. Consider two beings with great-making properties like omniscience, omnipotence, and goodness, but one exists necessarily and the other contingently. I suggest that the first has an excellence the other lacks. The seventeenth-century philosopher René Descartes proposed that the very idea of a perfect being was one in which the idea of essential (or necessary) existence was required in the same way that the very idea of a mountain requires the idea of a valley. There could not be a world of just mountains without there being some variations in height, with some landmass being higher (hence a mountain) than some other landmass (hence, by comparison, a valley). Similarly, to conceive of God is to conceive of a being whose existence is necessary, and (on this model) God cannot exist without existing necessarily.

PAT: I will challenge this momentarily, but I would like to hear the full argument first.

CHRIS: Very well. The second premise is as follows: God's existence is either necessary or impossible. The reason why this follows is that if the first premise is sound, then God is not the sort of reality that just happens to exist. In other words, God's existence is not contingent. Consider mathematics again: 1 + 2 = 3 just cannot happen to be true. It is either necessary or impossible.

The third premise is: God's existence is possible. This may be supported on several grounds. One might argue that we can consistently describe or imagine the existence of God. More modestly, the premise may be supported by the assertion that there appears to be no contradiction in the claim "God exists." But I prefer the more positive claim which earns some support from the three other arguments I offer. Evidence that something actually exists is evidence that it is at least possible that it exists. So, if the arguments I develop later in this conversation offer some reason to think God exists, then they also provide some reason to believe God's existence is possible.

The fourth premise is as follows: God's existence is not impossible. If that is true, then it follows that God exists necessarily. And the conclusion is that God exists.

PAT: Not so fast! I have some major objections. Let's begin with the first premise. Your definition of God as necessarily existing seems as arbitrary as defining a unicorn as necessarily existing. I have objected to your appeal to God as necessary earlier, but let me try again. I can define any term with the words "necessary existence" and come up with abundant absurd arguments.

If a unicorn named Adrian exists, it exists necessarily. Either Adrian exists necessarily or Adrian is impossible. It is possible Adrian exists. It is not impossible Adrian exists. Adrian exists necessarily, therefore Adrian exists.

CHRIS: My reply is that the concept of a unicorn—like the concepts of a magical island, or an elf, or a dragon, or horses—are all concepts of contingent beings. As I hoped to convince you earlier, the very concept of God is different but not (in terms of necessity) utterly unique. So, as you know, I think mathematical truths are necessary. Hence, my ontological argument is much more similar to the following argument than your unicorn line of reasoning.

If 1 plus 2 equals 3, then 1 plus 2 equaling 3 is necessary. 1 plus 2 equaling 3 is either necessary or impossible. 1 plus 2 equaling 3 is possible.

Therefore 1 plus 2 *not* equaling 3 is impossible. Therefore, 1 plus 2 equaling 3 is necessary. Hence: 1 plus 2 equals 3. However, the analogy with the unicorn is not completely off track. I would say that a unicorn being single horned is part of the idea of being a unicorn. Similarly, the idea of essential existence is part of the idea of God.

PAT: I insist again that mathematical truths are reflections of our concepts and language as opposed to some objective features of reality itself. I still believe you are simply defining God into existence by presuming God's necessary existence in premise one. There may be the appearance of an argument here but it is no more than if I were to argue that it is necessarily true in reality that there can be no male aunts on the grounds that "aunt" is defined as a female whose sibling has a child.

CHRIS: The male aunt example is interesting, though the impossibility of male aunts only holds because of the necessity of the law of identity. An example of "A is A" is the tautology "a female is a female." As I have sought to argue before, reducing necessity to language is problematic; while you hold that the statement that there cannot be a male aunt is only about language, I submit it is about an application of the law of identity.

PAT: But note how little work is carried out by attaching the term "necessity" or "necessary" to a concept; it does nothing to enlarge or shape the concept itself. So when I add "contingent" or "necessity" to "magician," I might be indicating the likelihood of your seeing the magician, but I do nothing like present a substantial argument that a magician (or God) exists. Words are tools we use to explore reality with thorough observation and testing. You, on the other hand, seem to use the tools of words only to explore mere words and not some necessary reality itself.

CHRIS: Two points in reply: First, I am using words to get at what I suggest is a genuine property (existing necessarily), and I suggest the concept of a God with this property possesses an excellence that would not be had by a contingent God. Second, a major part of the ontological argument is arguing that it is possible God exists, and because of this possibility one can rule out the impossibility of God's existence.

PAT: The true Achilles' heel of your argument is precisely this issue of possibility. You think God's existence is possible, though the burden of some of my arguments in our first and second conversations is that God's existence is impossible. Someone like me who thinks omnipotence and essential goodness are incompatible is offering good reason to think God's existence is impossible. The argument goes:

1. If God exists, God is omnipotent and essentially good.
2. If God is omnipotent, God can do evil; but an essentially good God can do no evil.
3. Therefore, there is no God.

And if this argument displays necessary features of God (e.g., it is *necessarily the case* that if God exists, God is omnipotent and essentially good), then this is an argument that God's existence is impossible.

CHRIS: I fully accept, in principle, the legitimacy of such lines of reasoning. You can launch arguments that God is impossible, and I believe I have successfully overturned them. (Recall my rejoinder to your Yahweh and Melkor thought experiment.) I see no contradiction in the concept of a God of unsurpassable excellence—and thus a being who is omniscient, essentially good, omnipotent, and so on—and think one can positively conceive of this divine reality existing, and thus secure the reasonable conclusion that it is possible that God exists.

PAT: This line of reasoning may work for you, but don't you see that unless you convince me that God's existence is possible, I am just as likely to think God's nonexistence is possible and thus necessary? Without a compelling argument that God's existence is possible, we have something that is indeterminate insofar as it is not proved one way or the other. So far, no one has proved Goldbach's conjecture is necessary (every number is the sum of two primes): it has worked for every number we have tried but we have no proof as of yet that it is necessary. So the possibility of God's existence might be in a position like Goldbach's conjecture, only not quite as strong; we do not know whether the concept of God has worked (or been coherent) in the past, and we have no *proof* of its possibility now.

CHRIS: I am fully willing to dispense with any reference to "proofs" when it comes to God or any substantial topic. I believe in good or bad arguments, and convincing or plausible reasons versus the mere appearance of good reasons. So, on the point of whether God's existence is possible, all I am aiming at is the conclusion that it is plausible (reasonable) to believe it—not that such a belief is irresistible and can be supported by compelling, undeniable proofs. I concede that different states of affairs may seem possible that turn out to be impossible. Perhaps Goldbach's conjecture might turn out to be an example of this. But we often can see that states of affairs that are actually incoherent may appear to be possible. To use a bizarre example, you might at first sight think there could be a barber who shaves all *and* only those who do not shave themselves, but eventually you see the contradiction: the barber cannot exist, for he would have to shave himself and not shave himself (a contradiction). I suggest that the concept of God, unlike our impossible barber, seems possible, and that any contradiction has yet to be unearthed.

PAT: I remain unconvinced. I believe the best you might achieve is an agnostic stance such as the conclusion "Given all I know, there *might* be a God, but there also might *not* be." Such a thesis is, however, too weak to give you a positive reason for embracing theism. Let's see if your next argument is better.

A COSMOLOGICAL ARGUMENT

CHRIS: Cosmological arguments hearken back to our first exchange and build on the concept of God as a necessarily existing reality. In that conversation, I asserted that the physical cosmos—and all that we observe and theorize concerning this spatiotemporal world—is contingent. None of this exists out of necessity. This is why, in part, the natural sciences must proceed by observation. There seems to be no necessity that, for example, photons exist, the earth began 4.5 billion years ago, there is carbon, water boils at 212 degrees Fahrenheit at sea level, and so on. We need observations to connect and explain the contingent objects of this world. The vast dispersion of physical particles in over a hundred galaxies does not at all appear to be necessary or self-explanatory. My question, then, is this: can the explanation of these things—the objects of the cosmos, and the cosmos itself—be solely in terms of other contingent things? I argue that this is not reasonable on the grounds that such explanations would amount to an infinite regress that would not truly be explanatory without the work of a necessary being—a non-contingent reality.

Some theists use this argument in tandem with big bang cosmology. They argue that astrophysics provides us with grounds for thinking that the cosmos had to have a beginning, and thus a divine cause, some 14 billion years ago. I do not take this route. Partly because I think the cosmological argument works not just in terms of positing a first cause in time, but in terms of positing a primordial necessary cause at *any* time. So, I believe that it is legitimate to ask why you or I or any other objects exist *now*. The mere fact that we existed a moment ago does not help us explain why we exist now without offering an account of how it is that we exist over time. Why should we—and indeed, the cosmos as a whole—exist and endure over time? Imagine we come up with an explanation in terms of other contingent objects. I exist because of the stable atomic structure of my body. One can then ask: why do these exist and endure over time? Perhaps we can add facts about the earth, sun, galaxy, micro- and macro-particles, but until we get to a reality that exists necessarily and can genuinely account for the existence of these contingent realities, we lack an account of my existence.

Consider three analogies: First, imagine we have before us a mirror with light in it. Where did the light come from? We are told that the light is a reflection from another mirror. Fine. Where did *that* come from? If the answer is another mirror and yet another, we will have no account of the light we see in the first mirror. In fact, without a source of light like the sun, which is an intrinsic source of light, we have no way to explain any of the reflected light.

Second analogy: Consider the meaning of "Omashimalaga" (a word I just made up). You ask for its meaning and I give you one-word answers with no external clues, no pointing, no syntax. "Omashimalaga" means the same as "Deyenan." Unless we come to a word you know or we can reliably signal what on earth I might mean, you will never come to know what is meant by the word "Omashimalaga."

Last analogy: You are holding a book. "Where did you get it?" you were asked. "I borrowed it," you responded. "Where did the lender get it?" you were then asked. No account of its origin will be given if you keep mentioning further borrowers into the infinite.

All these analogies point to the difficulty of accounting for contingent beings in terms of yet other contingent beings which require still further contingent causal support.

PAT: What kind of an argument is this? Is it a scientific argument? If so, then I know how to proceed. As I mentioned in our second conversation, in a case where we are trying to explain something—say the inheritance of characteristics—we posit some entity like a gene. We then know how to go about gradually describing and explaining its causal properties. But in your case I have no idea how to proceed.

CHRIS: I think your difficulty arises because you are treating the argument as an argument *within* the natural sciences, whereas the argument is *about* nature and the natural sciences. The argument is philosophical, rather than empirical with testable, reproducible factors. I am appealing to empirical observation and scientific theory to bolster the conviction that things in our contingent world have explanations with respect to other dependent causes. But the reason to go beyond dependent causes rests on the awareness of the perpetual loss of a complete explanation without a being that exists necessarily.

PAT: Your necessary cause continues to elude me. What are its properties? It appears to be unobservable and its only function seems to be to explain a contingent cosmos.

CHRIS: Not quite. I am offering a cosmological argument to expose a difficulty with naturalism (the thesis that nature alone exists), and to show some promise for going beyond the cosmos to account for it. Arguments from religious experience—as well as teleological arguments—provide a further body of factors or evidence that I believe is better explained by theism than naturalism. Also, while the cosmological argument does not offer repeatable experiments in which we may observe contingent objects being creatively conserved in existence by a necessary being, we can readily observe the relationship between causally dependent beings and see the need for a nondependent cause. Consider two causal relations: when I write, I typically use a pencil. The movement of the pencil itself cannot be accounted for without bringing into play a cause that is (in the context of explaining pencil movement) external to the pencil and self-explaining, that is, the pencil is being moved about by an author working on a manuscript about God. Or look at a water-skier being pulled by a motorboat. Looking only to the water-skier will not be complete; you need to look beyond to the engine of the craft pulling the skier. Indefinitely many cases can be multiplied to illustrate the logic behind the cosmological argument which presses upon us the fact (or reasonable belief) that the cosmos is not self-explaining.

PAT: Of course, in all your analogies or causal relations, we can come up with an account of motorboats (combustion engines, etc.) and authors (brain states, etc.) that all play a respectable role of explaining events in the cosmos. But what motivates the creative conserving power of this necessarily existing being? Why couldn't there be several of them? Does the necessary being act out of necessity or freely? Once you move beyond the cosmos to your necessarily existing being without a cause that brought it into existence, we seem at a loss to think clearly and confidently.

CHRIS: The cosmological argument is, as I said, advanced as a problem for naturalism and as one reason among others for the plausibility of belief in the existence of God. If the argument is being run on its own, so to speak, without recourse to other arguments with coordinated, cumulative force, then it might provide reason only to posit *at least one necessarily existing being.* Your Occam's razor might kick in to reason that we should not posit more than is necessary, but the argument itself does not rule out definitively multiple causes. When other arguments, like the one I will try next, are brought in, most theists build up a cumulative, comprehensive concept of God, and contend that God (the necessarily existing being) brings about and conserves the cosmos because of goodness itself. It is good that our cosmos exists rather than does not exist. Some theists have gone so far as to think our cosmos would be unworthy of creation and conservation unless it were the best possible cosmos. I do not. But I do think that in the teleological argument, which I will present shortly, we see a further difficulty with naturalism and reasons favoring theism.

PAT: Maybe the teleological argument will help, and maybe not. I still have other objections to your cosmological argument. You seem to be uneasy about positing an actual infinite number of causes stretching back indefinitely. Why? Imagine there was no beginning of the cosmos, and so for each year (or any other metric unit of time you prefer) let's assign a negative integer. Last year is −1, and the year before is −2, and so on. Why couldn't there simply be an infinite number of past years, each being explained by the year before?

CHRIS: As I mentioned before, I do not think the existence of something in the past can by itself account for its present or continued existence. Imagine we came across a massive rock. I ask you why the rock exists—why does it exist rather than a different object? The reply that the rock was there an hour ago does not answer this question, nor would an infinite series of affirmations that it has always existed.

PAT: I still think you are not taking seriously the nature of infinity. Let's say I concede, for the sake of argument, the point that the existence of objects over time requires further explanations. If the explanations go on infinitely, each explanation itself has another explanation.

CHRIS: But insofar as the explanations involve contingent objects, the regress is vicious and unhelpful, as though you can get out of debt by continuously borrowing or get a positive integer if you have enough negative integers. Moreover, even if you are able to get each explanation explained, there would still be no explanation of why this cosmos of infinite explanations exists rather than a different one.

PAT: But don't you have the same problem? You want to explain why this contingent cosmos exists rather than a different one—okay. You then appeal to the causal contribution of at least one non-contingent, necessarily existing being. I now want to know: is the activity of your necessarily existing being necessary or contingent? If it is necessary, then the cosmos exists necessarily and is not contingent after all. But if the activity of the necessarily existing being is contingent, does not *that* need to be explained? Maybe you risk your own infinite regress. If your effort is to account for contingency and you can do so only by appealing to necessity, what you need is a necessary cause. But if this is to be God, then God must create necessarily, and thus not freely. If you believe God is free, creation must be contingent and you still have your problem with contingency. Hence, you have a problem: either God (or some such being) created the cosmos and is not free, or God's creation is contingent and thus not explained.

CHRIS: I submit *the causal contribution* of God as the necessarily existing being is contingent—God was not and is not *compelled* to create and conserve a cosmos over time. And yet, the one who undertakes this contingent act of creation is itself a necessarily existing reality. You confuse the ideas of the necessity of *God* with the necessity of *God's acts*. We theists in the classical traditions hold that God freely created out of goodness, or for the sake of goodness, and in so doing, the creation is explained on the grounds of teleology or purposive intentional agency: the goodness of the cosmos is a reason why it exists. So the regress of explaining the existence of the cosmos ends—not arbitrarily, but in the explanatory, purposive agency of a necessarily existing being. At this point we are getting into the teleological argument.

PAT: Before doing so, allow me to summarize where we diverge. You treat questions like "Why is there a contingent cosmos at all?" or "Why is there this contingent cosmos rather than a different one?" as legitimate, independent quandaries. But then you appeal to a cosmos-explaining being, a kind of Super-Creator who is said to have a property of necessarily existing and freedom to produce *our* created order rather than another. Let me pose this query: which came first, your questions or your concept of a God? I suggest there is a sense in which if you did not already have the concept of a cosmos-transcending being, the question of why there should be a cosmos at all would not arise.

CHRIS: I do not concede the point. I think the question of why the cosmos as a whole exists naturally follows from our everyday and scientific practice of raising questions and requiring explanations of things within the cosmos. But even if the concept of a contingent cosmos emerged simultaneously with the concept of a reality that could explain the cosmos, why would that be a problem? Imagine the concepts "murder" and "murderer" emerged simultaneously (which they probably did; I can't imagine one without the other). This fact should not dissuade us from criminal investigations. . . .

PAT: Ah, but in the case of murder and murderers we are dealing with observable phenomena. Perhaps a better analogy would be if we both were called upon to account for a lion's fierceness. Let's say I explained it in natural terms involving mating, reproduction, competition, and so on, but then you asked: "What about the property of fierceness itself?" The mistake you would be making involves looking beyond the data provided in a natural explanation to some super-explanation we have no independent reason to suspect. Your mistake is akin to someone who wanted to see a college. The person is shown all the buildings, students, professors, staff, alumni, founding documents, and so on. But then the person complains: "You haven't shown me a college; you have only shown me the parts that make up a college." The mistake of thinking the cosmos as a whole needs to be understood as such is the same mistake made by a person who thinks a college is more than its parts. I see no reason to feel compelled to go beyond cosmic explanations to explain the cosmos.

Consider your analogies to the mirror, the meaning of terms, and the book. In our cosmos we would not accept as a good explanation that I see light in mirror A because it is reflected from B, which comes from C, and so on ad infinitum. I would need to appeal to a light-generating source. Agreed. Let's say that source is our very own star: the sun. Once I get to the sun, I might explain it in terms of 15 billion years of dust and gas, but at no point do I feel compelled to go beyond the cosmos. The same thing holds for understanding the meaning of terms or explaining the origin of books, for example, we can account for the invention of paper in China, which eventually made it into Europe at such and such a time, and so on. If you are stopping your explanation of the cosmos in terms of a powerful, ultimate teleological reality, why cannot I just regard the cosmos as my ultimate frame of reference? Neither my cosmos nor your God requires a further explanation. Fine. Occam's razor should then lead us to prefer my cosmos to your God.

CHRIS: But keep in mind the massive difference between your concept of the cosmos—which remains contingent—and the concept of God which is non-contingent. Let me fill this out and then move to the teleological argument. The concept of *being human* is the concept of something contingent. After all, *homo sapiens* have only been a stable species for around 120,000 years or so. The concepts of *the sun* and *the earth* and *galaxies* are similarly contingent realities. But, the concept of God is one that contains existence in the sense that *what God is* (a maximally excellent being) entails or involves *that God is*. The same is true with respect to necessary truths such as that a triangle is three-sided, wisdom is a virtue, and $2 + 2 = 4$, each of which is true whether or not human beings, the earth, the sun, or galaxies exist. As with the concept of God, these entities are such that their very nature is necessary existence. Your analogy with the college does not work. A college (like a corporation or nation) is composed of a host of parts, including legal charters. Once all the parts, including the set of rules that defines the membership in the college, are cited, then one has identified the college. Just as each part of the college is contingent, so is the college as a whole. When looking for an explanation of *why* there is a cosmos at all (or a college), simply adding up contingent causes will not achieve a non-contingent, necessary being whose agency can account for the cosmos.

PAT: As you know, I still find your very concept of a necessary being or necessary truths in general unsatisfactory, as I believe mathematics, geometry, and definitions are features of language. There may *seem* to be a problem here because the existence of language is contingent and these truths are necessary, but I treat the necessary here as relative to language. Given that there is language, and given stable uses of terms like "triangle" and so on, the necessary truths follow. In any event, let's go on to your teleological argument.

A TELEOLOGICAL ARGUMENT

CHRIS: Very well. The cosmos is an ordered, complex whole or universe. I realize that the assertion I am now going to make is controversial and deserves its own debate in the next conversation, but here goes: I submit that the existence of our complex, stable, life-sustaining cosmos with the emergence of consciousness and moral and religious values is itself *good*.

For all the ills—the human and nonhuman-animal suffering—it is still better that the cosmos exists rather than does not exist. Given theism, the goodness of the cosmos is a reason why it exists. Theism thus offers a reason why this cosmos exists as a good cosmos rather than not, whereas your naturalism is unable to offer such an account.

PAT: I shall argue that the state of the cosmos—its value—actually does more to support naturalism than it does to support theism. You are quite correct that, given naturalism, there is no good purposive, intelligent, force that created and conserves the cosmos for the sake of its goodness. My argument will be twofold: if there were such a good purposive force, it should have done better work. This is the so-called problem of evil. Alternatively, a naturalist account of the cosmos can offer an account of how life, consciousness, and values have emerged from valueless processes. On this front, evolutionary biology offers a brilliant account of the cosmos that utterly bypasses any need for a good purposive cause.

CHRIS: The problem with appealing to evolutionary biology as a suffi-cient answer to the teleological argument is that the very laws of nature that constitute biological evolution themselves require explanation. Why is it that our cosmos is such that we are in a stable, contingent condition that allows for the origin and sustaining of life? An account of *how* life-forms evolve is not ipso facto an account of why there is a world of in-organic and organic matter.

PAT: Again, you are on to your point about ultimate explanations that take us beyond observation. The beauty of evolutionary biology is that we begin with something very simple, explaining the complex and emer-gent in terms of simple components. You seem to begin where we end; that is, you begin with the concepts of intelligence, power, knowledge, and goodness. But we seek to explain the origins of intelligence, power, knowledge, and goodness. You simply help yourself to the very things for which we ought to account. In the words of Bertrand Russell, you achieve all the benefits of theft rather than through honest labor.

CHRIS: I suggest a different portrait of you and me. Neither of us are thieves. I believe we both may be seen as starting with two general types of explanation: intentional, teleological explanations versus non-intentional, non-teleological, causal explanations. I assume you grant me that, in the case of humans, teleological explanations make sense (we do things for goals and values), and perhaps this holds true for some nonhuman animals. We also both agree there are non-intentional, non-teleological accounts, as when we appeal to thermodynamics in explaining temperature exchanges. I submit that given a non-teleological structure, the radical emergence of conscious life, ethics, and so on is the unintended—in a sense accidental—byproduct of an impersonal nature. I will not deny that this is possible, but I do propose it is not expected or likely. Given theism, however, it is expected or likely that an all-good, intentional being would bring about a good cosmos.

PAT: I will challenge your appeal to the goodness of the cosmos in the next conversation. I agree, in principle, that if the cosmos was the sort of creation expected by an all-good Creator, you might offer a wider, more comprehensive explanation of the cosmos except for one thing: time. Given an infinite period of time and endless physical stuff (matter and energy), I suggest that it is inevitable that there would emerge a cosmos that looked like the creation of an intelligent, teleological reality. Perhaps you have heard the story of the monkeys? If you have an infinite number of monkeys with an infinite number of computers over an infinite amount of time, eventually they would type all the works of Shakespeare. Actually, the example may be simplified: given infinite time, a single monkey on a single computer would inevitably complete all of Shakespeare's work. Your teleological argument only has a modicum of plausibility if we posit finite time, as well as accept the premise of the goodness of the cosmos which I will soon challenge. The role of time is a key element in my naturalist account of life. If the earth is only several hundred million years old, I have a problem accounting for the vast numbers of species on this complex planet. But if we accept current cosmology, the earth is 4 billion years old and the first living organisms emerged 3.8 billion years ago. Darwinian evolution can provide a successful account of the gradual formation of bio-diversity through differential reproduction, heredity (with genetics), and fitness.

CHRIS: Let me reply to your current objection on two fronts. First, given infinite time it does not follow that every logical possibility will occur. It is logically possible, given the truths of atomic theory, that my hand can pass through a wall without impediments. But it is far from clear this would ever occur given even infinite time. Or imagine the infinitely many different possibilities with respect to our own world: given infinite time, is it reasonable to think there would one day be a world just like ours except that the Berlin Wall had one less brick in it? I do not think so. Second, if the appeal to infinity did allow us to discount the appearance of purpose, wouldn't it conflict with what most of us reasonably believe? For example, I hope you believe that the last book you read was written intentionally, but given infinitude and the assumption that all logical possibilities would inevitably be released, shouldn't you suspend judgment, because, after all, it is logically possible this book manuscript was randomly generated or typed by tireless, infinitely hard-working monkeys? Or, shelving the infinite monkeys, isn't it possible the book was randomly generated by some non-conscious, non-programmed computer?

PAT: I think you are missing my point. We don't treat the monkey or random generator hypothesis as live options in accounting for books, because these are never observed or encountered producing Shakespeare's work or any books. What I was trying to get to is the idea that the positing of infinite time and chance may be no worse of a hypothesis than your theism. If theism and naturalism (given infinity) are equally explanatory, Occam's razor gives us reasons not to posit anything outside the cosmos.

CHRIS: And my point is that the time-and-random-occurrence hypothesis simply fails to account for what would be likely given theism. Even with respect to evolution, I believe theism provides a better overall framework to account for why there is and continues to be a cosmos in which there are stable laws. Theism is able to better explain why this fundamentally good cosmos exists and continues to exist rather than naturalism. Let me try a different analogy. Imagine an innocent person is about to be executed by a firing squad made up of seven seasoned soldiers. They all take aim and miss by yards. Two hypotheses present themselves: (1) they all miss by accident; (2) their missing was intentional either on the part of the soldiers or of those who rigged the rifles. We naturally see the execution of an innocent person as bad, and so we have reason to think good persons have positive reasons for preventing the execution. The cosmos, I suggest, is similarly something we have reason to believe a good Creator would bring about.

PAT: I will challenge that shortly. In fact I will argue that the cosmos is far more like an unjust firing squad than a group of soldiers who refuse to execute the innocent. My thesis will be that if there were an all-good God, there would be few, if any, firing squads ever.

AN ARGUMENT FROM RELIGIOUS EXPERIENCE

CHRIS: Okay, so let me briefly sketch my fourth argument for the belief in God. I submit that there is widespread testimony of the experience of a transcendent, sacred reality. Sometimes these experiences are explicit and stand out against normal, secular experience. But more often than not, there is testimony of a sustained experience of the divine, a reality that is describable in personal terms as good, wise, knowing, and the like. I myself have such a sense of the divine. It is not overwhelming or undeniable, but it is as real, or as apparently real, as my experience of love or kindness or justice. I have felt this sometimes quite explicitly in Quaker meetings, ashrams, Christian churches, Jewish synagogues, and mosques, and in almost all settings, urban or rural. This apparent disclosure of a divine reality is, I suggest, further evidence of the existence of a divine reality.

PAT: It may not surprise you, but I am skeptical of the quality of your evidence. I think your argument faces at least four challenges: First, there is tremendous religious diversity you seem to be ignoring. I am inclined to think that the religious experience of, say, the truth of a religion like Islam would be evidence against Christianity and so on. A Christian's experience of the divinity of Jesus does not go well with a Muslim's experience of God's nonhuman transcendence. Second, there seem to be ample ways in which naturalists such as myself can explain away the phenomenon of religious experience: fear of the unknown, a desire for mercy, forgiveness, control over one's life, and so on. This can be force-fully filled out when you take seriously the role doctrinal training plays in preparing believers to have these experiences. We seem to not have experiences of Jesus in cultures where Christianity is not present. Why? I think it is more likely that the Christian training and education actu-ally *produces* the experiences themselves than it is probable that Christians just happen to have an impartial, untainted experience of God. Third, there is a radical gap between what is experienced or could be experi-enced and what is reported. No one can possibly knowingly have an ex-perience of an omniscient being. How could you ever know a being is omniscient? Maybe the being you seem to experience is very knowl-edgeable—but omniscient? Or omnipresent? How on earth, or beyond this earth, could you tell? Finally, we now seem to be able to induce re-ligious experience through pharmaceuticals and other modes of impact-ing a subject's brain states. Occam's razor once again gives us reasons for favoring a natural explanation of the phenomena.

CHRIS: I will reply to each objection, but I suspect that the status of the argument from religious experience will need to be revisited after dis-cussing the problem of evil and taking stock of all the evidence available (in the fifth conversation). So, at present, consider these brief replies. Religious diversity is less divisive than I think you imply. Classical Ju-daism, Christianity, and Islam are quite interwoven and share many of the same elements in their reported experience of the divine. Judaism and Islam deny God became incarnate as Jesus, but Muslims recognize Jesus as a holy prophet and both Jews and Muslims recognize a kind of embodiment or specific manifestation of the divine which, while not an incarnation, hints at a modest compatibility. So, Jews have looked to wis-dom (sometimes pictured as a person) as a specific disclosure or manifes-tation of God and Muslims hold that the Qur'an is the temporal em-bodiment of the eternal Word of God. Each of these religions, and some forms of Hinduism, speak of the God (Yahweh [or YHWH], Allah, or Brahman) revealed experientially as good, compassionate, and powerful. Hindus sometimes recognize multiple embodiments of the divine. Kr-ishna, for example, is an avatar of Vishnu, who visits and encounters us in the form of a human being. My point is that religious experiences of the divine are quite broad and do not have the sharp incompatibility you suggest. Historically, Hindus have proposed that Christian experiences of Jesus are authentic experiences of the divine, as Jesus is (like Krishna) an avatar. And some Christians have held that the God of Jesus is active in Hindu and other religious contexts. I suggest that God has many names.

PAT: But don't you wind up with a very watered-down concept of the divine? After all, think of the vast number of polytheists—believers in multiple gods—among other varieties. The more names you allow for God, the wider you must conceive of God. Your view of God becomes less particular or specific, and more unwieldy, containing multitudes.

CHRIS: Maybe. I see an overall unity and convergence in much of these traditions, but however broad my concept of God, don't you still have a problem accounting for the significance and scope of religious experience from a naturalist point of view? Aren't there widespread experiences that at least appear to disclose a transcendent reality not accounted for in your secular frame of reference? Let me briefly reply to your other points and then let you have the last word, though I suspect Liz wants to get a word in too. So, on to your second objection: perhaps naturalism *can* explain why so many of us experience what we think is divine but why *should* one be skeptical? Occam's razor should not be allowed to cut us off from what appears to be a challenge to naturalism if the experiences are multiple, convergent, and coherent. You are right about there being a difference between religions—and let's debate this further in conversation five—but for now I will simply claim there is profound compatibility. You can appeal to fear and the desire for consolation to explain away religious experience, but I recommend caution here because someone can easily reverse such appeals and claim that the reasons behind some denials of God involve fear, an inordinate desire for autonomy, and so on.

PAT: I agree that attributing ill motives to each other will get us nowhere. But let me clarify my challenge. I propose that we naturalists can provide a good explanation as to why human beings appear to experience a transcendent, divine reality. There is great survival value in positing a caring, benevolent deity (or multiple deities) who will provide for you in this life and the next; such a belief probably helps people face suffering and death. Perhaps the belief in a benevolent Creator helps motivate the development of tool-making, industry, and agriculture: people reason that if God or the gods delighted in fashioning the natural world, so should we. And an appeal to God probably has had a role in stabilizing order in some societies. Given all this, and the fact that those who can convince others that God is "on their side," why shouldn't there naturally evolve tendencies to report encounters with this deity?

CHRIS: The more natural the explanation of religious experience, the better. Why shouldn't God use natural means to perpetuate an experiential awareness of God?

PAT: I will not rule that out, at least for the sake of argument. And yet, the persistent problem you have with natural explanations is as follows: an apparent experience of some state of affairs (seeing a yellow object) is only evidence that the state of affairs exists (the object is yellow) if you would not have the experience of the state of affairs if matters were otherwise (the object is not yellow). So, let's say there was a powerful yellow light on in a room such that any object at all that was blue or green or orange would appear yellow to you. Under these conditions, you should not take the apparent experience of seeing a yellow object in a room as evidence that the object actually is yellow, for it could just as well be any color whatsoever. The analogy with the experience of God is as follows: there are many natural reasons to explain why persons would seem to experience God even if there is no God. Therefore you cannot use reported experiences of God as evidence of God's existence.

CHRIS: Let me back up a bit. When I said that the more natural the explanation of religious experience the better, I meant that I welcome accounts that allow for the possibility that we can have genuine experience of the divine. Just as we are naturally receptive to food and air, I believe we have a natural tendency to be receptive to the divine. Your yellow room analogy can help make my point. Right now, most of us with normal vision can reliably identify yellow objects in sunlight. We rely on our observational experiences because we have no positive reason for thinking there is a powerful yellow light distorting our vision. Your earlier principle about states of affairs is itself open to challenge. If we adopt your principle, all our observation experiences would be undermined. After all, it is possible (however bizarre) that we might all be in the Matrix. Our brains might all be electrochemically stimulated such that we merely think we are awake and engaged in dialogue. We could, in other words, have all the experiences we are having now and yet our experiences would be utterly unreliable. I suggest, then, that your principle needs to be replaced by something like: If one has no positive reason to believe an apparent experiential observation of X (colored objects or God or whatever) is distorted (e.g., you have no positive reason to believe the objects are subject to bedeviling light conditions or you have no independent, powerful reasons for embracing naturalism), then it is reasonable to see these apparent experiential observations as authentic experiences of X. In a phrase, our apparent experiences of X should be treated as trustworthy or innocent until proven otherwise. If your case for naturalism is not decisive, then I think you have to be open to the evidence that religious belief may provide.

PAT: Well, I don't claim to have *decisively demonstrated* the truth of atheism or naturalism, but I think I've brought up enough reasons to make an honest, impartial inquirer strongly inclined to naturalism. And once someone grants that naturalism should be given *greater initial plausibility*, then I suggest that reported religious experiences lose their innocence. In any event, what do you say about my third and fourth objections?

CHRIS: Your third point about the difficulty of a subject knowing he or she is encountering a being that is omnipresent, omniscient, and so on, is forceful. Here, all I am claiming is that religious experiences give us reason to be receptive to a divine reality: a different set of arguments would need to kick in to get all the divine attributes. I would use a combined ontological argument for divine excellences like omniscience along with an appeal to revelation claims. The latter refer to claims in sacred scriptures that we have some reason (perhaps based on religious experience or miracles) to think of as genuinely revelatory of the divine. This might involve propositional revelation whereby God discloses truths about the divine nature. Such disclosures need not be seen as oracular auditions whereby a prophet functions as a secretary writing down divine speech. These disclosures could come about by inspired, divinely-guided human thinking and imagination, backed up by a vivid experience of God's leading presence.

Finally: the brain and pharmaceutical argument. Let it be granted that we can produce "mystical states" by creating micro-seizures of the temporal lobes of the brain. Imagine such seizures bring subjects to think they are in the presence of an awesome, personal, sacred, good reality. Would this in any way diminish our confidence in such a mystical awareness? Not at all. This is partly because, according to the classical theism I defend, God necessarily exists and cannot be absent in any part of the natural world. God is not some object like the Taj Mahal that you can only see if you are in Agra. As such, there is no way for a naturalist to set up a control case and electrochemically induce a subject to experience God when God is absent.

Consider an analogy with logic. Imagine that when someone has certain types of seizures they realize the number 7 is prime. Imagine a world where this is even the only time people have such an awareness. The (imagined) fact of explaining mathematical experiences this way would not or should not lead us to doubt 7 is prime. Obviously more would need to be said to fill this out, but I hope to have made a start.

PAT: Your last point brings up again the issue that has bothered me from the beginning. Your God hypothesis posits a necessarily existing, teleological being that exists inevitably (non-contingently) so we cannot undertake experiments by which to test the hypothesis. If I want to test someone's mathematical skills, we can check her reasoning. If I want to see whether someone's vision is reliable I ask whether she can accurately report when certain objects are present or absent. But a necessarily existing omnipresent reality cannot, by definition, be absent. This observation alone does not show that religious experience is unreliable or reliable, but I hope it shows that appealing to religious experience is far more problematic than it appears. In testing our senses, there must be ways in which we can independently verify whether our senses are reliable. So, for example, imagine I seem to see some water on the horizon, but then when (if there were water) I would be soaking wet and I am not, I conclude that some refracted light has caused me to see a mirage. In experiencing God, however, you have to rule out the possibility of my merely seeming to see (or experience) God. But surely there must be cases when God is not the proper object or stimulus of my experience.

CHRIS: Yes, I think cases can arise of *mistaken* experiences of the divine, or where the cause of one's experience may be deviant. Dividing authentic from inauthentic experiences must draw on many factors. Take a reported experience of God's blessing of an emperor. Is this the outcome of mass psychology? Is the reported experience of the divine in accord with other reports? Is the experience itself compatible with what we have independent reason to believe philosophically? If the ontological argument gives me some reason to believe in God's essential goodness, I have some reason to doubt the report of a religious experience that God is evil or God has blessed an evil emperor.

PAT: But note how different, and more difficult, it is to articulate experiences of God rather than ordinary perceptual experiences of the world around us. You simply lack the stable framework to clearly divide the reliable from the helter-skelter results of an overactive imagination. Let's return to your claim that the experience of God is as natural as our receptivity to food and air. With food and air, we have the possibility of confirmation over time with multiple physical senses and common sense. It is obvious that food and air exist, otherwise we would not survive. We can cross-check our observation of ordinary physical objects, but none of this can be carried out with God.

LIZ: I suspect Chris will again point out that it is in principle possible that *all our sensory observations could be mistaken* (as in the Matrix) and this would not be detectable through "cross-checking." I also suspect Chris would argue that the framework for distinguishing credible from spurious reports of religious experience is no more difficult than distinguishing experiences in other areas of life involving values. Cases may arise when it is not clear when an experience of love or beauty or courage is authentic. Differentiating reliable and unreliable experiences may require subtlety, time, the comparison with other experiences, and so on. This may sound too subjective or unscientific, Pat, but in my view there are areas in life when science is not enough, and there is an inescapable subjectivity in some of our most important reflections. In any case, I am not as interested in defending Christ as I am in pointing out why I part ways with both of you. You seem over-convinced that our ordinary perception is doubt-proof, or immune to skepticism, while

Chris seems to accept the basic reliability of our senses and then to argue, by analogy, that if we trust our ordinary sensory perceptions, we should trust what seems to Chris to be our apparent experiences of the divine. I take a different approach: the divine is profoundly *other* than ordinary, terrestrial, cosmic phenomena.

I do share with Chris, however, the question about why this cosmos exists, but in my version of the question I broaden the scene: Why does *everything* exist? Haven't you felt the urgency of such a general question? I have, and I suggest that the only possible answer to the question is a reality or being that is beyond "everything." Once you get beyond every "thing," you begin to get an idea about who or what is truly behind the cosmos and—most relevant to our exchange—beyond human concepts and thoughts. The supreme cause of everything is not like something in the cosmos that we can compare with other things. On my view, God is radically *transcendent*. Chris places too much emphasis on the *immanence* of God.

PAT: I am afraid I cannot follow you. If something is beyond "everything," that "something" is no thing or, to be succinct, nothing. Nothing is not something. It cannot create, think, be conscious, or do anything. I therefore find your position either completely puzzling or I see you as a member of my party, namely, denying there is a God.

LIZ: In denying God is a thing, I agree that I begin to look rather like I am an atheist. I do not have a problem with that. But if I am what you call an "atheist," I am still deeply in awe and reverence to the God beyond being, and I live my life in reference to the One I address through prayer and meditation as the holy God. One of the reasons why you two might want to take seriously my philosophy of God will emerge at the end of the next conversation. You see, both you and Chris seem to picture God as an agent of some kind—a moral subject who might compare well or badly with human beings. So, you and Chris might raise questions about whether God should intervene with world events. But intervention into something implies that the one who may intervene exists alongside of the situation or in an arena in which the intervention can take place. But if God is the creator of *everything*, then God is not included in the "everything" and thus God is not a thing that exists alongside of the creation. God is *behind* "everything." Perhaps you will see some appeal of my position after you both address the problem of evil on your preferred terms, in which Chris will affirm God is a good Creator and agent in the cosmos, and Pat will deny it.

QUESTIONS FOR FURTHER INQUIRY

1. The ontological argument is often formulated (as it is in this dialogue) as an argument from possibility to necessity. Are there other arguments of the same form, and do you find them more or less convincing than an ontological argument for theism?

2. Cosmological arguments are sometimes formulated by an appeal to a principle of sufficient reason. It has been proposed that for every actual state of affairs there must be a sufficient reason for that state of affairs obtaining (a sufficient reason why the state of affairs is actual). Some philosophers use this principle to argue that without appealing to the activity of God (a necessary being) we will never have a sufficient reason for any concrete contingent state of affairs. One of the justifications for this conclusion is that an infinite series of sufficient reasons is vicious and will never suffice as an explanatory option. Do you find the principle of sufficient reason plausible? Do you think there can be an infinite series of causes in which each event in the series is explained by some other event, and on and on? If each event was explained by other events in the series, would it still make sense to ask why there is an infinite series of events?

3. Teleological arguments for theism are sometimes of the form assumed by Chris in the dialogue involving an inference to the best explanation. Chris's argument is, essentially, that given theism, the existence of a good cosmos has a better explanation than it does given naturalism. But sometimes teleological arguments proceed by analogy, that is, the universe resembles objects we know to be designed, such as watches, thus it is reasonable to believe the cause of the universe resembles (in part) the designer(s) of a watch. Construct an argument from design by analogy and assess its merits. You may find it useful

to compare a cosmic argument from analogy with other arguments from analogy.

4. Under what conditions, if ever, do you think that an ostensible
   (apparent) experience of God would give you a good reason to
   think the experience is of God?

NOTE

1. From *Sherlock Holmes: The Complete Novels and Stories* by Sir Arthur Conan
Doyle (London: Bantam Books, 1986; "The Science of Deduction" was first
published in 1890), vol. I, 108.

FOURTH CONVERSATION

If God Exists, Why Is There Evil?

> If [God] is willing to prevent evil, but not able? Then he is impotent. Is he able, but not willing? Then he is malevolent. Is he both able and willing? Whence the evil?
>
> —David Hume (d. 1776)[1]

PAT: My argument against the existence of an all-good God will be brief. Is murder evil? Or rape? Or torture? Or genocide?

CHRIS: Absolutely.

PAT: Why?

CHRIS: Because they involve the violation of human life.

PAT: And do you think that if you could prevent a murder or a rape, you should do so? If you had the power and opportunity to do so or to prevent torture or genocide, don't you think you ought to do so?

CHRIS: Yes!

PAT: Well, if there is an all-good God, this God is either not all-powerful or not all-knowing. If, on the other hand, God knows of the evil, can prevent it, and does not, God cannot be all-good. What especially bothers me about your belief in an all-good God is that if you somehow

77

manage to justify all the evident evil and suffering, then you risk losing sight of the fact that murder, among other acts, is profoundly evil. So, for example, if you were to justify God's allowing evil for some greater good, why shouldn't you, Chris, allow such evil for a greater good? Consider an analogy: surely it is permissible, possibly even obligatory, to inflict some pain if that creates greater good. None of us will deny the goodness of parents who take their child to a dentist or surgeon to be healed when there is no alternative to a painful medical treatment. We would readily see that while the surgeon may hurt the child in order to cure her, this hurt is not a matter of grave moral harm. Just as well, then, if it is permissible for *God* to allow evil (and the magnitude of evil is breathtakingly tragic), why shouldn't *you* allow the evil?

THE GOODNESS OF A CREATOR OR CREATURE

CHRIS: You raise a powerful argument with roots that go back to ancient Greek philosophy. The problem I have with your reasoning, however, is that you seem to treat God as a human agent like you or me. But when thinking about the goodness of God, one is thinking about the goodness of a Creator and not just of a creature. So, in my view, God has created a cosmos which is fundamentally good. It is fundamentally good insofar as evil is a damaged or disfigured good, whereas goodness is not a disfigured or absent evil. You would not have evil unless you had goodness. The sickness, injury, or brokenness of a human or animal is (under this model) parasitic on the good. I adopt what is traditionally called the *privati boni* (privation of good) theory, according to which evil involves the deprivation of a good. It is good that there are stable laws of nature, and vast numbers of stars and planets. It is good that there is organic life, human and nonhuman consciousness, sensation, movement, emotions, and desires. I further believe it is good that there are creatures such as ourselves who have genuine freedom in our responsibility for each other's welfare. I also believe there are obvious evils, including ways in which people use their freedom to murder, rape, and torture. I see the problem of evil as a genuine problem, for I also see evil as something that is a profound violation of the will and nature of God. Most of the theistic religious traditions see evil as the object of divine wrath or sorrow. To commit evil is to commit an act abhorrent to God's essential goodness. The way I suggest we see the problem of evil, then, is as follows:

> Is it plausible to think that an all-good God would create a world in which there are profound goods as well as evils, some of which are the result of the misuse of free creaturely acts, a world in which it is every creature's duty to prevent murder, rape, torture, genocide, and so on whenever possible? This world is one in which the evil that occurs is the object of divine sorrow or wrath, as the evil is an aberration and disfiguration of nature and a violation of God's will and nature. God does act in the world to destroy some but not all evil (through prophets, incarnations, theophanies) and God works to redeem or deliver all creatures from evil in this world and a world beyond this one. Moreover, in the world created by God, the existence of God is apparent to some by experience and insight, but not to all people at all times. The goodness of the Creator is, rather, progressively revealed over time in this world and the next.

Once you fill out such a picture, we are looking at a different kind of question or dilemma than you introduced. I believe the answer to the above question is yes; I think it is plausible that behind the enormous evils of this world, there is a good Creator-redeemer.

FREEDOM, GOOD, AND EVIL

PAT: You have certainly moved our conversation to a different setting, but it isn't one that I find the least bit plausible. I find the whole concept of an afterlife absurd; I have a deep problem with your concept of freedom. I reject the *privati boni* theory and I think your effort to distinguish between the ethics of a Creator and the ethics of a creature is deeply worrying. You seem to be arguing that the overall state of affairs of a cosmos with good and evil is compatible with God's goodness. But isn't it good for us (Creator or creature) to do what is *best* under the circumstances and *to do the best of our ability*? Surely we can imagine a world in which free creatures did not misuse their freedom. There is no logical absurdity in imagining a cosmos of happy creatures who are cordial, respectful, compassionate, and content. Why would God create a cosmos such as you describe rather than one which lacks such profound evil?

CHRIS: I grant that there is no logical or metaphysical impossibility of a cosmos of consistently good, free creatures. But there is no way God or anyone can *guarantee* that creatures who have genuine freedom will always exercise that freedom for good. As you know from our second conversation, I have not fully made up my mind on God's relation to time, but I am inclined to the view that omniscience cannot include foreknowledge of what future free action will occur. In creating persons with authentic freedom, God cannot fix how persons will use that freedom. There are two difficulties with your charge that God should bring about the best outcome. First, whether or not free creatures are good or the best depends on the creatures themselves, not the Creator. Second, the concept of *the best creation* seems itself suspect, like the concept of a *greatest possible number*. Imagine God creates a cosmos brimming over with happy creatures. What might be better? Creating more happy creatures.

PAT: Let's slow down here. Earlier I objected that your concept of God is akin to the concept of a greatest possible number. If I grant you that God can be unsurpassably great and this involves no conceptual problems, why not a creation that is unsurpassably great?

CHRIS: "Greatness" is relative to kind. On this point, Liz seems right. What makes a horse great is different from what makes a book great. In the case of God, as I argued in our second conversation, the concept of being maximally excellent or unsurpassably great picks out a unique reality, or at least a concept of a unique, holy being. God's greatness is more like the completeness of a figure (a circle having a natural upper limit of 360 degrees) rather than the completeness of an indefinite series of units. With respect to the total number of created things or universes, there may be all sorts of excellences but not, I think, unsurpassable excellence.

PAT: As you know, I don't accept your value theory, so I do not concede the point. Let me focus, though, on the kind of cosmos we do witness— setting aside for the moment whether this is or should be or could be the best of all possible worlds. While we have earlier assumed that freedom involves an ability to do one or more acts, I think such a concept needs to be revisited. Why not hold that someone is free if she does what she wants? And conversely, someone is not free when she cannot do what she wants?

CHRIS: Okay, that does seem like a kind of freedom.

PAT: We can fill it out a bit further to avoid bizarre cases of hypnotism and brain control. In doing so, I propose that *a person is free if she can do what she wants; she wants to do what she wants; and she is not being deliberately manipulated by an external agent.* Here, then, is why I think your appeal to freedom is unsuccessful. Why can't God create persons who want to do good and are actually successful in doing so? This would not be a case of *manipulating* persons; it would instead be a case of *creation.* God simply makes creatures who are successfully free and oriented to the good.

CHRIS: I am inclined to think that while such a creation contains a kind of freedom, it is not the deep moral freedom that defines our responsible action. Some philosophers have proposed that deep moral freedom involves acting in favor of goodness when one could do otherwise. Such free good action is genuinely up to the agent. The good creatures you propose simply cannot do other than the way they are created to act. Their own freedom is already fixed.

PAT: But fixed only in one respect: these creatures may be determined (or created) to do good, but what kinds of goods they do may be fully up to them. Why not create a cosmos in which creatures may choose only among a rich variety of goods? Some theists believe angels are like that or the saints in heaven. Very well, then, why not begin with everyone like an angel or a heavenly creature?

CHRIS: My response is a bit complex. I think a world of essentially good beings is good, but I also think a world in which persons have deep moral freedom to be either good or evil is itself good. Having choices only among a variety of goods is not an arena in which creatures have very much responsibility for one another. If I am so made that I can only choose how to love people, my love itself seems something that is not of my own making or something for which I can take credit. Now I do not have a problem with angels. In my view, there can be all sorts of forms of intelligent, purposive beings with different levels of power, knowledge, and goodness and, as you know, I reject the thesis that purposive beings must be human or even corporeal. There are angels in different strands of Judaism, Christianity, and Islam, as well as angel-like spirits in Hinduism (the deva) and Buddhism. I do not think all these angelic beings are essentially good; there is, after all, a tradition that there is a malevolent spirit (Satan, the Devil, Beelzebub) who was created good, but turned to evil. In any case, if God and angels are essentially good (and I believe God is essentially good), then God and angels can do no evil. In this, they have an excellence humans lack. But free creatures who are capable of love as well as hate, compassion as well as malice, have a good that God and angels do not have. And it is worthy of a good Creator (I suggest) to bring into being and conserve a cosmos in which there are moral choices among beings who are not essentially good.

PAT: Why create us at all? If God and angels and creatures that are created only to do good have an excellence, why create humans and other creatures who lack such an excellence?

CHRIS: Because goodness is not and should not be limited to the highest excellence. You may know the expression "perfection is the enemy of the good," which is often aimed as a warning to people who have perfectionist tendencies that paralyze them. This is the sort of paralysis of a student who will not pass a course because she will not submit a paper until it is (in her estimation) perfect. Most of the philosophical theists I follow are inspired by the idea that the excellence of God lies in God's self-diffusive goodness, or God's creating a rich variety of goods. In Latin the old phrase is *bonum est multiplex* (good is multitudinous), whereby divine love delights in the *bonum variationis* (the goodness of diversity). My thesis is that it is good that there are free creatures who can fail or succeed in love, even if it is also true that it is good that God and maybe lesser beings (like angels) who are essentially good exist; however, your allusion to saints in heaven and the challenge of why God didn't just create heaven calls for a brief comment.

The whole concept of heaven in theistic religions is the concept of a realm of restoration and consummation of a lifetime of spiritual growth—and perhaps a blend of failure, then growth, failure again, then further formation. In many religious traditions—certainly in traditional Christianity—heaven is supposed to begin now. (I believe that is the meaning behind the proclamation attributed to Jesus that "the kingdom of heaven is within you." See the gospel of Mark.) So "heaven" refers to a dynamic development or a state into which one moves. As such, it would be odd to think of a heaven of saints as something God could create at the beginning. It would be like someone suggesting at the Olympics that the race begin at the finish line, and we put to one side the race itself, or proposing that one could hear Big Ben toll four times without having it toll twice.

PAT: You may be right about the concept of heaven, but your metaphor raises my basic problem with your Creator. The cosmos is not set up for a fair race in which we have an equal shot at winning heaven. People are born with horrible disfigurements they do not deserve. Some are born with severe tendencies to be cruel. And to claim that people are permitted to suffer so that others may help them seems a horrific justification. You have not made this point explicitly, but you seem to imply that it is good for there to be a world in which there can be costly, valuable love. If it is permissible to allow evil in order to bring about great good, maybe we should relax our efforts at preventing birth defects. This returns to the logic of my original objection: if it is permissible for God to allow evil, why shouldn't we?

CHRIS: God forbid. Recall my (perhaps unsuccessful) effort to argue that we need to distinguish considerations of value when it comes to being a Creator versus being a creature. Yes, if there is a God, then this God has created a cosmos of great danger in which God allows that which is abhorrent to God's nature and will. A single, undeservedly suffering child is something in radical conflict with the God of theism.

PAT: That's my original problem. If God is all-good, why should God allow for such harm to God's purpose and nature? If you're invoking freedom again, I want to directly challenge your position as well as take aim at the *privati boni* thesis.

How valuable is freedom? I suggest it is only valuable when it leads to something good. So, freely aiding a vulnerable, innocent person is good. But what if what is at stake is something evil? Is freedom good when someone freely injures a vulnerable, innocent person? I would say that the freedom here makes the action even worse than if the evildoer was not free. Freedom's value is only in proportion to the good or ill it leads to. If the only freedom you had was to do something trivial and uninteresting, then the freedom itself would be trivial and uninteresting.

Rather than look to freedom as a great good, I prefer a more down-to-earth approach of seeing how people use the powers they have, whether it is to bring about great suffering or joy. And when taking that into account, one can see the unsatisfactory character of the *privati boni* thesis. Consider a case in which a person is suffering massive, undeserved pain. This is a *positive* evil. I suggest that the vast amount of positive pain and suffering gives us excellent grounds for concluding there is not an all-good, all-powerful God.

CHRIS: I actually do think that freedom is a positive good and so I will try to counter your first point and connect my counterargument with a defense of the *privati boni* thesis.

The person who uses his freedom to harm an innocent person is, I suggest, misusing a power or virtue (I am using the term "virtue" to re-fer to a good or excellent power). This is a case when someone uses a good power that is (in my view) created by God to promote goodness and perverts this power to bring about a twisted and unnatural end. It is unnatural insofar as the act violates both the nature of the one harmed and the wrongdoer's divinely intended human nature. I take your point that if we compare two cases—one in which someone commits an ill act freely and another in which the act is involuntary, or not as free—the first has an ill the other lacks. But the ill or disvalue is significant because the wrongdoer misused something of value he should have used for a greater good.

As for suffering, your point is substantial. Debilitating, undeserved pain is, I agree, not merely the absence of good (the way in which dark-ness is the absence of light). But I do uphold a *positive* view of nature it-self and of the person undergoing the suffering. When a person or or-ganism goes into intense, unrelieved suffering there is a sense in which the nature of the person or organism is being deprived of the good that fulfills its nature. The evil of the suffering is due to a corrosive deprivation of health and what is good. In this sense, the privation of evil thesis still seems right to me.

SUFFERING AND THE NATURAL WORLD

PAT: I do not think you'll find much help in appealing to the positive value of nature itself. The natural world is filled with violence, predation, and immense, incalculable suffering. Moreover, think of cases where the very nature of organisms seems bent on destroying organisms, as with parasites that seem to be programmed merely to destroy their hosts painfully. Sure there can be cases of parasitism where there is symbiosis ("living together") and mutualism (organisms enjoying mutual benefit), but there are also infectious agents that ravage human and nonhuman life to no purpose whatsoever. The natural world is shot through with entropy (the dissipation and destruction of life) and death. Think of the enormity of nonhuman animal suffering, the vast offspring of all manner of living things consumed by others. What sort of essentially good God would have created such a fabric of pain?

CHRIS: To respond to your objection requires a whole philosophy of nature, pain, and animal consciousness. I personally believe many nonhuman animals with brains, nervous systems, and pain behavior (they avoid injury, seek sustenance, and so on) do suffer and can experience pleasure and contentment. And, in the cases of apes and dolphins, I am highly disposed to see them as persons or person-like creatures. But as we find creatures without a well-developed prefrontal cortex and a right neocortical hemisphere, I am less and less sure we find full, self-conscious suffering. In human action, we sometimes find emotional, physiological responses to pain, but without full consciousness, and so we cannot decisively attribute full consciousness simply in the presence of some ostensible pain behavior. You and I can engage in purposive activity without full self-consciousness. This happens when I sleepwalk.[2]

PAT: But surely you don't want to go so far as to suggest that nonhuman animals are like sleepwalkers! In fact, I wake up to full self-consciousness if I happen to bump into a wall and feel pain.

CHRIS: The pain that seems expressed by innocent animals in the course of nature is heart-wrenching. I do not wish to underestimate it or be callous about it, but I do want to note that we are not in a position to be able to accurately gauge the level of animal feeling as the organisms get more remote from our physiology. Occam's razor might have some legitimate work to do when we examine primitive forms of life. If the behavior and anatomy of some organisms can be accounted for without full-blown consciousness, we should not posit it.

PAT: It seems like you appeal to Occam's razor when it is in your interest to do so. I'll take the opposite view. If an organism acts like it is suffering, why not assume that it is? Doesn't this reasoning conform to your defense of religious experience according to which we should trust appearances unless we have positive reasons not to?

CHRIS: In most cases I do trust appearances and I do acknowledge animal suffering, but in cases of assessing nonhuman animal emotions and feelings where the physiological basis for consciousness is less and less developed, I think we need to be cautious. In any case, *I affirm and do not deny animal consciousness.* And, as it happens, I am deeply opposed to the way we humans mistreat animals through intensive confinement and utter disregard for their well-being. (As an aside, I am not a vegetarian, though I do try only to use animals that are raised cage-free and without cruelty.) Getting back to the problem of evil, I propose that for the great majority of the nonhuman-animal world, we need a more ecological and evolutionary perspective. A world of only herbivores, with no carnivores or omnivores (some Christians see the original creation in Eden of *Genesis* as such a vegetarian realm), may be imaginable, but it is hard to imagine an animal world as we see it in nature with animal sensations, cognition, and motion without predation. The whole process of one animal consuming another represents a natural, fundamentally fitting and good process of transferring energy and sustaining life.

PAT: The concepts "transforming energy" and "sustaining life" sound so clinical; they only thinly disguise the appalling agony involved. So what if a world lacked the animal properties that go along with predation? I could live with a world where animals lacked horns, their teeth were less sharp, and their eyesight and hearing were less well-tuned. I suggest that you should be concerned that your God raises animals with cruelty. Where is the great good of a wolf falling upon a deer?

CHRIS: It's a good meal for the wolf? I actually favor an ecology that balances populations and in some cases I endorse the repopulation of wolf packs in order to impede deer populations. In ecology, I think we need to focus on the good of species and not just that of individual animals.

PAT: Why not do this with humans too? You seem to be on a slippery slope here. If you are fine with culling a deer herd through predation, why not the human species? It may seem outrageous even to contemplate such a question, but there are some ecologists today who so value the earth (or what they call the biosphere) that they regard humans (at least at our present and growing population) as a defect, a kind of cancer. My point is that if you focus on the good of species, why not go further and focus on the good of all species and the entire earth-ecosystem? Why shouldn't humans be treated like deer in assessing the overall good of the planet?

CHRIS: With humans, we have cases of clear self-awareness and personhood. I doubt deer are people, though I value individual deer (i.e., they should not be subject to human torment for the sake of entertainment) and deer as a species. I do value the good of the whole planet and biodiversity, and I believe we humans should change our environmentally irresponsible action (excessive pollution, our annihilation of other species), but I recognize the deep value of *persons* and thus the difference between human persons and other species. It also happens that I so value the *wildness* of nonhuman animals that I tend to oppose zoos unless a zoo serves clear, beneficial educational purposes or preserves a valuable species that is otherwise endangered. But in your view, predators should probably go into zoos and be fed vegetarian diets. Your own outlook tends to be pitted against the natural world. Given your position, shouldn't we humans police the natural world to prevent pain and predation?

PAT: You've got me wrong there. I am not opposed to predation in the wild. I agree it is natural. But what I have been arguing is that if there is a God who set up the natural world, why did this God allow for so much suffering? Because I do not think there is a God, I do not blame God or nature or anyone for predation. But my argument is with you: surely evolution is a pretty wasteful way of creating the world! Why so *much* horror?

CHRIS: I am not sure you can maintain the view that nature contains horror (avoidable suffering) and not do everything you can to oppose predation. Let's say there is no God. Fine. If you believe (a) predation in nature involves great suffering; and (b) this suffering should be prevented by beings with the knowledge and power to do so, then (c) in the absence of other more stringent duties, you ought to police nature using whatever technology you can (perhaps sterilizing some deer to prevent overpopulation rather than rely on predation or hunting). I submit to you that "c" collapses into absurdity. The natural world contains suffering, yes, but also enormous good. And I count as good very basic things like sentience, breathing, movement, agility, and so on.

PAT: I think those are good as well, and of course I am not going to endorse "c." I was arguing that from the standpoint of what you have been referring to as the Creator, there seems to be a great deal of gratuitous, avoidable suffering. We are not gods or God, so we will never have to puzzle about whether to make nature one way or the other. Even so, in your personal practice you are committed to meat-eating "without cruelty." In making this commitment, you have employed a higher standard for animal well-being than you attribute to God. Surely the enormity of animal and human suffering must at the very least fuel an uncertainty about God's existence in the majority of people who reflect on the suffering in this world.

EVIDENCE AND VALUES

CHRIS: Actually I think some kind of uncertainty about the existence of God is actually good. If we are truly to have freedom apart from God, there has to be some cognitive remoteness from God. That is, if God's existence were overwhelmingly apparent to us, we could not disbelieve or disobey God. Disobeying an evident omnipotent force would not be a live option for anyone keen on self-preservation. Freedom in relationship to God requires a certain hiddenness on God's part.

PAT: Your position involves so much of an appeal to that which we do not know. Obviously I grant that God's existence is not obvious; quite the opposite, for I think it is near obvious that God does not exist. But note the oddity of the following exchange: Imagine your friend believes there is an invisible cat in the room. You complain that you don't see the cat, and he replies: Of course you do not! If you saw the cat, it would not be invisible. The problem with your stance is that you are appealing to what you do not see (i.e., the afterlife, God's existence). I think it is far more reasonable to argue that we do not see God or the afterlife because neither exists than to argue that we do not see them because they do.

CHRIS: But keep in mind the context of my defense. I am not quite in the position of your friend with the invisible cat. I believe there is a significant, but not overwhelming, body of evidence for the existence of God. This emerges from considering the contingency of the cosmos, its apparent purposive value, and religious experience. Evil, in my view, is a problem. It is a problem for God, as well as other beings, for it involves a violation of God's will and nature. Moreover, it is never good or justified for evil to occur.

PAT: But in your view God allows or permits evil. God could have elected not to create at all. Or, once evil occurred, God could have allowed the cosmos to cease to exist. But instead, if you are right, God must find that there is something good about there being a cosmos like ours, complete with all its horrors.

CHRIS: Yes, and I'd like to use your phrase "something good about there being a cosmos like ours" to press my point. Evils can occur which should not, and yet it is better not to destroy those who undertake the evil rather than to work to redeem those who commit the evil. Imagine, for example, a murderer. The person may well deserve to be executed and, putting the point more forcefully, it might be the duty of a magistrate to carry out this execution. Nonetheless, imagine the killer confesses, repents, seeks to compensate the family of the victim, and commits him- or herself to a lifetime of heroic, nonviolent acts that save others from harm. In such a case it may be that while justice requires executing the murderer, there is a principle of mercy according to which the magistrate can still be good in the course of setting aside strict justice for the sake of redeeming the killer.

PAT: I have multiple problems with this concept of redemption. If the magistrate really should (as a matter of justice) execute someone, then not doing so is unjust. I myself oppose the death penalty, but if I am wrong and capital punishment is not merely morally *permissible* (meaning it is not wrong), but morally *required*, then a just magistrate ought to impose it. Are you conceding to me that the God you believe in is unjust?

CHRIS: I am claiming that God is not restricted by justice or subject to justice alone. Mercy is a force that can and should temper or qualify justice—or sometimes even set justice aside—for some great good.

PAT: *Being unjust* versus *setting justice to one side* seems like a distinction without a real difference. I suppose you think that setting aside justice for the sake of mercy is not being unjust, but this seems to me a dangerous game. Violating justice is violating justice—period, irrespective of motive. Let me advance my overall point with a parable. Imagine you came to a kingdom in which murderers, rapists, and torturers go unpunished. You do not see the landlord interfering very much, if at all, to prevent these horrors, even though it is obvious that punishment and prevention are required as a matter of justice. Imagine further two people in that kingdom: one concludes that the landlord must be working in ways we cannot see to redeem the wicked, while the other concludes that the landlord is good and enfeebled, bad, or nonexistent. Isn't the second person far more reasonable than the first?

CHRIS: Given what we know of landlords, and given that the advocate of the good-yet-hidden landlord had no positive reason to "keep the faith," I agree. But the case at present is different. God is no mere landlord; rather, if God exists, God is the maker of all land, people, space, galaxies, and so on. God is able to act far outside what we can observe now. And, if I am right, we are not utterly in the dark about God's nature.

PAT: That is precisely where we are. If you do not like my landlord parable, consider another. Imagine a parent places his child in the woods. Maybe the parent thinks the child will develop all sorts of virtues by being alone and battling the elements, confronting her fears, and so on. But imagine the child cries out for the parent and she only hears the wind and the howls of wild animals. Surely a loving parent would not subject his child to such a horror. The parent would reveal his loving care and protect the child.

CHRIS: I think that on the level of human parentage that is correct. Divine "parentage" is different, for it involves a cosmic context no mere human parent can construct. But let me work with your parable a bit. In the view I am proposing, there is some good for God's hiddenness or, to put the point quite directly, it is good that there are atheists. Being an atheist allows for certain goods not available to the confident theist who is convinced that an all-good God will preserve him or her in life. Let me explain.

Imagine you and I observe a child trapped in a burning building. It is likely that either of us would succeed in getting the child out alive, though at the cost of our own lives. I actually believe in an afterlife. I charge in and, after rescuing the child, perish. I have paid a huge price. I will never have this life again. But I nonetheless also believe that my death is not utter and complete annihilation. Imagine you enter the building, rescue the child, and then perish. Unknown to you, there is a God who loves you and will not let you perish utterly, but you will still have a glory or good that goes beyond mine, for you gave all that you believed you had to give.

PAT: Glad to hear that atheism has its virtues, though in our fifth conversation I will amplify virtues other than simply heroic deaths! But while we are on the topic of the afterlife, which seems to play a key role in your defense of God's goodness, I now wish to challenge your appeal to what we do not know. I think we have very positive reasons for thinking there is no afterlife, and if an appeal to the afterlife is an essential part of your defense of theism then this next argument may expose the Achilles' heel of your position.

CHRIS: Carry on!

THE COHERENCE AND VALUE OF AN AFTERLIFE

PAT: In our first conversation, you sought to argue that there is more to human life than brains and behavior; there is also consciousness or subjective experience. I hold that there is conscious, subjective experience, but it turns out that this actually is the very same thing as brain processes. I doubt I convinced you of my argument that correlation of consciousness with brain states is evidence that the two are identical.

CHRIS: Correct. I think one may have a full conception of conscious subjectivity quite apart from brain states and vice versa. This is very different from your other examples of identity, such as water and H_2O; in that case we may see that water is simply H_2O. I further think one can conceive of a person becoming disembodied or switching bodies, and I believe we can conceive of fully functioning bodies without there being any consciousness. In the terms that one often uses these days, I believe, as you know, that zombies are possible.

PAT: And, as you know, I think that such "possibilities" are akin to fantasy or fairy tales. In the realm of fairy tales, anything goes. But for now, I will not try to rule out these options in principle. My concern is not presently with what is abstractly possible, but with what is plausible. Even if you are right that consciousness is not identical to brain states, all evidence points to the conclusion that consciousness *depends* on brain states. Damage to parts of the brain brings about impairments to consciousness. The relationship of consciousness to the brain is highly complex, but we have achieved a reasonable, general picture.

Now, I would say this is good evidence that the conscious states *are* the brain states. The alternative is intolerable, for in any alternative theory you would have a kind of dualism, with consciousness (or the mind or soul) as some kind of nonphysical process or spooky substance interacting with the physical world, and I find this preposterous. Such a dualism is utterly against science. But even if dualism were correct, I hope you will agree that the evidence is overwhelming that consciousness is radically dependent on the brain. It is because of this evident dependency that it is unreasonable to think persons or consciousnesses survive the demise of their bodies.

CHRIS: Before I reply to your last point, let me register my conviction that we actually do have interaction between consciousness and the brain. And your worries about the interaction of the physical and nonphysical are not (in my view) impressive, partly because the very nature of causation in the physical world itself seems quite open-ended. There no longer appears to be a scientific prohibition against action from a distance (objects can causally affect others without spatial contact or the mediation of other objects) and the principle of the conservation of energy does not appear to rule out interaction. If physical objects can have basic, not further explainable causal properties, why not nonphysical objects or processes? But, yes, I do take your point about the profound dependence of consciousness on the brain, though I do not think this in any way establishes that persons or consciousness ceases *in nihilum* (into nothing) at death.

PAT: I think it does. My reasoning is straightforward. Just as the lack of a brain and brain activity in a fetus is good evidence that a fetus at very early stages of development does not possess any consciousness (the brain does not develop until six to eight weeks after conception), the ceasing of brain activity or (more dramatically) the annihilation of the brain is evidence of the annihilation of consciousness. The probability of surviving the death of the body is zero.

CHRIS: I have a few replies. Let me first take note of the fact that some religious traditions believe in a physical resurrection. Many Christians in fact think that the afterlife will be realized when God resurrects their bodies at the final stage of human history. You may find this hopelessly superstitious, but if there is an *omnipotent* God, perhaps one should not rule this out as having some plausibility. There is also a group of theists who believe God can re-create a person after she has ceased to be. In this view, a human person is said to have a gap-inclusive existence: an identity over time that includes a gap during which the person ceases to be.

I do not rule these out as options, though my preferred position is a dualist one, according to which a person is not (strictly speaking) the same thing as her body. Yes—during a healthy life I function as my body and to see me is to see my body. But in severe illness and eventually death, matters change. As I increasingly lose control of my body, it may be that my body can function only as a container for my consciousness, desires, and intentions. Finally, at death, I think my functional identity with my body is gone and all you will have left of my earthly life is a corpse.

PAT: You have given me some further background about how you might be able to conceive an afterlife, but no real reply to my plausibility argument.

CHRIS: Fair enough. Given this background, though, what evidence do I have that I have ever witnessed the annihilation (the utter and complete ceasing to be) of a person? I think it is certainly reasonable to believe that once we have evidence that someone's brain has no EEG readings, that their heart has stopped, and so on, we have reason to believe the person is no longer conscious *there*, for that body's embodiment of a person has ended, but is the ending of an embodiment ipso facto the absolute ending of a person? This is something we simply do not see or knowingly observe. Picture two houses that seem visually identical:

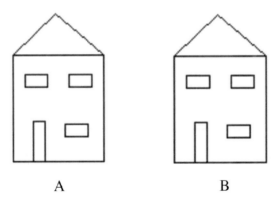

A   B

I inform you that one of the houses is empty. The other house has a party going on, but everyone is hiding so you cannot see them. How would you know which is A? You wouldn't, until some distinguishable change occurred, such as you spotting a partygoer looking out a window. Something similar is going on with the afterlife. Picture a scene in which someone dies and his or her soul (or mind or consciousness) comes to be with God, versus a death after which the person ceases to be and there is only a corpse. To us—or to an outside observer—the scenes are like the houses: indistinguishable. It would not be indistinguishable for the person who died if there is an afterlife in accord with some of the great world religions. Actually, Christianity depicts the afterlife in terms of many houses that one may come to explore (John 14:2). I witnessed the death of my father three years ago. I did not see him enter a heavenly mansion, but I would not have seen this empirically if he had. So, the fact that I did not witness it is no evidence that instead of his soul or consciousness being with God, my father was totally annihilated at death.

PAT: I am sorry for the loss of your father; I lost my mother two years ago. It gives me no pleasure to argue that both our parents have ceased to be, but for us to deny this is simply to avoid reality. Maturity involves putting to one side our childlike hope that we shall all live forever after this life. Consider my argument once again: Surely you treat the absence of a brain and EEG readings as evidence that the fetus is not a person at, say, one week. If you do that, doesn't consistency compel you to reason that at the cessation of EEGs or the destruction of the brain the person has ceased to be?

CHRIS: I do treat the absence of a brain as evidence of the absence of a person, but I do so with some hesitation. Hinduism and Buddhism both uphold a belief of reincarnation, according to which the soul has a prior life (and thus a prior death). I happen to think that reincarnation does not occur, but I do think it is possible and I am open to evidence in its favor. If, for example, ostensible memories of past lives were not better explained on naturalist grounds, I might well embrace such a belief. But because I currently do not believe in reincarnation and my belief in a good God leads me to believe in an afterlife, I treat the absence of a brain as evidence of a consciousness or mind or soul (or the person) not yet existing; and while I treat the loss of a brain as evidence of biological death, I do not see the latter as evidence that God or nature annihilates persons, making them cease to be.

PAT: I understand the logic of your position but I hope you understand mine. I agree that failing to observe the continuation in existence of the soul of a dead person does not by itself amount to observing that this did not occur. Just like failing to observe a party in figure B is not evidence there are no partygoers in the house. My skepticism comes in on the level of doubting whether the continued existence of a soul (or mind, etcetera) makes sense, given what we know. We know that the dependency of consciousness on the brain is thorough. Setting aside our exchange about out of the body experiences, we, as a matter of common sense, treat biological death as the termination of persons.

CHRIS: Let me try to move our conversation forward by focusing on values. One way it might make sense to you to think of an afterlife is if you consider the value of human persons. Think of a person you know who died in very old age. Perhaps his body collapsed from natural causes. We might naturally speak of the person as having had a full life. But consider the following: has the full worth and vibrancy of the person himself been used up and expired? Imagine that you have an ability to restore this person to a level of fitness, concentration, and strength so that he might continue to have a life that is animated by loving goals and creativity. If you loved the person, wouldn't you undertake such a restoration? If so, doesn't this suggest to you a distinction between the value of bodies (which will run out or die by so many years) versus the value of persons? Speaking personally, if I had been in possession of great power and was able to restore my father (who died at ninety-five years) into a vibrant state, I would have. The belief that a loving God would sustain persons beyond death is not an immature, childish response to death, but the natural outcome of believing in an all-powerful, loving God. Love plus power would act restoratively through death.

PAT: I have several difficulties with your imaginary scenario. First, it seems to involve magic. We simply do not have such age-reversal powers. Second, while I can sympathize with anyone who would enable a damaged youth to be restored, isn't there a natural endpoint at, say, a hundred years, when enough is enough? Third, you seem to be entertaining a dangerous dualism between the person (a durable good) and his body (something that is defective because, eventually, it breaks down).

You offered all sorts of praise of the natural world. Assuming you truly value the natural world and you do not posit an afterlife for nonhuman animals, why posit one for humans?

CHRIS: I will reply in reverse order. First, in proposing that a person's value is not exhausted by his or her body, I am backed up by common-sense. A person's body is made up of cells that are radically regenerated over the years. While much of the brain matter and bone marrow that you had as a child in kindergarten is the same, your body today is radically different. The value of persons is far more important than the value of your body at any one time. For a person to value his body at any time is to value something that will not be with him in several years. To say that a person's value surpasses his body does not attribute any defect to the human body; human bodies simply wear out. But isn't it the case that there is something that transcends the body when it comes to the value of persons?

When it comes to nonhuman animals, it seems like desiring ever-lasting youth for all animals is a desire for magic, and my original thought experiment of revitalizing a being may seem like an exercise in wish fulfillment when it comes to dogs and cats. The fact, if it is a fact, that non-human animals do not have an afterlife because they are not persons, does not by itself denigrate nonhuman animals; however, believing that this is the only life they have may well intensify our desire to care for them.

PAT: Why not conclude that if human beings did not have an afterlife, we would value them more? Limitations can cause us to *intensify* our concerns. If I have the opportunity to talk with you only five times, our conversations shall be far more focused than if we might talk a hundred times. Doesn't the idea that a human person's life is limited magnify or intensify our concern for others?

CHRIS: I think it is *because* we value humans *as persons* that we are led to believe that a loving, powerful God would not limit human persons only to this life. I do grant, however, that some limits can magnify our concern. Perhaps we should live each moment as if it may be our last. One may still do this and yet reasonably hope for more moments and more life together.

Let me step back a bit to clarify the difference between us. Both of us value the natural world (even if we have different views of the good or ill of animal behavior), but when it comes to evident evils, naturalists who deny libertarian free will have to believe that all evils seem built into the very structure of the cosmos itself. The Nazi Holocaust, for example, could not have failed to occur, given the laws of nature and antecedent and contemporaneous causes. But on the grounds of theism and libertarian free will, we can affirm that such evil is contrary to the very *telos* or purpose of the cosmos itself.

ABSOLUTE EVILS AND HOPE

PAT: Your invocation of the Holocaust does not bode well for your entire position. I will grant that if we adapt your limited theistic framework, the Holocaust was not foreseen through omniscience and the Holocaust itself involved some exercise of freedom by malevolent creatures. I will put my argument in a single sentence: The Holocaust is so profoundly evil, it should have been prevented using divine omnipotent power. I know of no conceivable reason it was allowed to occur, if in fact there is an all-good, all-powerful God who could have prevented it. Hence, the Holocaust stands as a decisive ground for disbelief in God. In fact some (but certainly not all) Jewish philosophers have come to see the Holocaust as a definitive reason for abandoning theism, and for subscribing to a form of Judaism that only recognizes as divine the vulnerable, valuable being of other persons.

CHRIS: From a theistic point of view, the Holocaust is never justified; it remains a case of unparalleled sacrilege against the divine will and nature and the sacredness of human life. As such, there would be something deeply suspect morally in naming different goods that would in any way warrant its occurrence. In the face of what might be called such *absolute evil*, we theists must (in my view) preserve the recognition of its absolute evil while also maintaining that the only way in which there might be some redemption (albeit no justification) that comes through such horror is if there is an omnipotent loving God. Given naturalism, the death of 9 to 11 million Jews, homosexuals, Gypsies, and others in the genocide is the absolute annihilation of each person with (as you said earlier) zero percent chance of surviving death. Given theism, a loving, powerful God can bring it about that death does not have the last word, and that these people did not perish irrevocably. Faith in such a God is perhaps most pronounced among religious theists who hold that God suffers in and through the world. God is not an absent landlord or forgetful magistrate. Christians, in particular, think that the life of Christ testifies to such a God who seeks to actively redeem the worst victims, and bring the malignant agents to justice.

PAT: But none of this makes sense to me. What might an afterlife offer? It cannot be compensation, for we defined an absolute evil as something that can never be warranted; by implication, this means that the wrong committed can never be put to one side because of some future good. To think otherwise would be to justify one person abusing another so long as he or she afterward gave the victim immense bliss. I grant that in naturalism, the loss is irrecoverable, but isn't that a reasonable belief to have, namely that an unspeakable, irreversible evil has been unleashed? Your proposal that only an omnipotent and loving God can redeem the lost may be used by you to urge us to hope there is a God. But to me, this would amount to hoping there was an all-powerful agent to blame, for no matter what rescue takes place after death, the Holocaust's evil is absolute.

CHRIS: First, I am not in any way thinking of the afterlife as compensation. It would, however, stand as an arena for the possibility of redemption. In this life, we do tend to think certain crimes and damage is unredeemable (that is, there can be no recovery) and many people think the death penalty is justified. Perhaps people can deserve death, or capital punishment can be justified as a way of preventing more crime. But if theism is true, we need to allow for the most radical kind of "thinking outside the box" because we are considering a Creator God with omnipotent redemptive powers.

How might there be healing, regeneration, and life after an "absolute evil"? Imagine death is not the end and "on the other side" the Nazis and their collaborators face the truth of their actions, their character, and the horror they created. What might happen? You may not care, and in a short lifetime of even a hundred years, there may not be sufficient time for someone to lament, to put to death their former selves by renouncing their wickedness, to be regenerated. But let's imagine time is not an issue. Let's say the wrongdoer has a thousand years. A million. A billion. There need be no upper limit if we allow for omnipotent, good power.

Also, given omnipotent, good power, can we close the door on the different levels of possible transformative experiences? Kubler-Ross (a specialist in the study of near death experiences) once conjectured in relation to the Holocaust that one fitting end for a wrongdoer would be to relive experientially the lives of all those he or she killed to know what evil was done from "the inside."

I do not personally have definite views on such possibilities, but the position I defend is that there are good grounds on the basis of multiple arguments to believe in a good, purposive God. The created order contains the deepest, most splendid goods as well as the deepest horrors. Can an all-good God have created this cosmos in which there are profound goods and ills, some of which are due to our free action? Can one believe that God does act in history—through Jesus, Lao Tsu, Gandhi, and other sages—to overcome evil, and God acts beyond death to redeem wrongdoers and those harmed? I believe so, and am even more convinced of two further points: we are not in a position to answer this question negatively *and*, contrary to your earlier point, there are grounds for hoping that there is omnipotent redemptive power. Let me briefly speak to both points.

On the first point, we are only able to reach a negative answer to the question if we are in a privileged, extraordinary position. If someone fails to see why an all-good God would conserve a cosmos like ours in existence, this failure would only be evidence that there is no reason if you would see the relevant reason. In other worlds, failing to see X is evidence that there is no X only if you *would* see X if it were there. Take a silly example. You see Pierre behind a fence.

Does Pierre appear not to have a mustache? No, because you would not see it if he had one. You are in a situation where he neither appears to have one nor appears not have one. So, *his not appearing to have a mustache* is not the same as *his appearing not to have a mustache*. The example is silly, but the point I am trying to make is that if there is an all-good God, we cannot count on our being able to grasp all the reasons behind divine action. So, failing to see why God allows evil does not alone establish or legitimize the idea that God has no reason.

My second point is that while I believe being an atheist has some virtue or allows for some virtues that would not be possible for a theist (the reverse is also true, as I shall argue in our next conversation), theism does provide grounds for a hope that tragedy is not the last word in human history. I am not putting in a pitch for wish fulfillment, or suggesting one should be a theist because it permits a more positive view of history, but I do want to highlight an important aspect of theism: it speaks to a genuine love of people and the world. It is not out of hatred of wrongdoers or fear of death that I have developed my views in our conversation but out of a love for the created order.

PAT: I will not challenge your self-assessment and trust you will not question mine. I do not reject theism because I want death to be final and for there to be no redemption. I simply think the evidence either does not support theism or, in the case of observed evil, is against it.

I take your point that failing to see X (whatever it is) is only evidence against the existence of X if you would see X if it existed. In the matter of good and evil, I think that if there is an all-good God, this God would be more evident. Maybe God likes atheists, but frankly if there is a God I would prefer *not* to be an atheist. I say this not because I think an all-good God will punish nonbelievers, but because I want to believe what is true. If atheism is false, I do not want to be an atheist. In my view, an all-good God would (and should) reveal why certain evils occur, and the absence of such a revelation is evidence that there is no God. The case of Pierre is comparatively better than the case of God. In your example, I may not know whether he has a mustache but I at least can see that he exists. In the case of God, I not only can't see why God should allow for evil, but I cannot see that there is a God at all (good or bad).

LIZ: I have followed this exchange with interest, but now I need to step forward, opposing both your positions. I think you, Chris, got off to a good start in pointing out the difference between a Creator and a creature, but then you and Pat did not seem to go far enough. Both of you still seem to assume that, if there is a God, then God is a moral agent. Both Chris's drawings of houses and Pierre, and Pat's lament that God would inform us all of God's reasons seem equally unsuccessful. I must say, I am not persuaded by Pat that we are entitled to regular divine disclosures (Can you picture how God would let us all know why this or that accident occurred?), nor am I impressed by Chris's appeal to creative freedom. The problem is that God is not a kind of thing that can be compared morally with you and me. I do think of God as good, but not like Chris who uses the term "good" analogously to the way we would speak of a good parent or landlord.

PAT: Once "good" is taken out of the realm of goodness in human relations I have little grasp of what might be meant by calling God good.

LIZ: I think God is good in the sense that God is the creator of the goodness of the cosmos. Sorry to disappoint you, Pat, but I am rather drawn to the privation account of evil. Because God is the author of everything and the cosmos contains evil, it is a legitimate question to ask why there is evil. But in a sense, I do not see evil as a created thing. "Evil" refers, in my view, to the forces that corrupt and destroy creation. It may be that any material world with complex, interrelated organisms will inevitably be a world in which there are forces that threaten creation. I do not know. But I do know that if God is the creator of the *goodness of the cosmos* and because God is not a moral agent, the problem of evil is no longer an objection to the existence of God.

PAT: But if God is a Creator, then God is an agent. And if God is an agent, shouldn't God's actions be assessed just like any other agent?

LIZ: I see the creation by God not so much as a matter of agency, but of a unique, unparalleled causation. The creation—everything—comes into being and is sustained by a God who is not a thing even if our language implies God is some kind of substance. If God is not part of "everything," God is not measurable (either philosophically or morally) the way anything else is measurable.

PAT: I am not sure you can make these sorts of claims, Liz. Once you think "God" is beyond everything or beyond existence and being, I fear your notion of God has ceased to be intelligible.

LIZ: I agree that my talk of God has ceased to be intelligible in our ordinary categories, but we should expect nothing else in terms of the radically transcendent God.

CHRIS: Perhaps Liz is right, but if so then it seems the appeal to hope and redemption or deliverance from evil seems undermined. If God is beyond *everything*, how might we even begin to see how God might love and deliver created persons from evil?

PAT: If Liz is right about God being beyond *everything*, there is a problem here. But I think you, Chris, face problems of your own. I have some deep misgivings about how God might be revealed or incarnate or redeem creation. Let's take this conversation into the heart of some specific religious beliefs.

QUESTIONS FOR FURTHER INQUIRY

1. Some philosophers have held that "good" and "evil" are polar terms and that one cannot make sense of one without the other, like hot and cold, thick and thin, short and tall. What is your view? Do you think there can be evil without good? Can there be good without evil?
2. Some raise the claim that our world is not the best possible world. Can there be a best possible world?
3. What, in your view, is the nature and value of freedom?
4. Do you think the process of evolution, with its predation and massive, perpetual loss of life, is unworthy of being created by God?

5. If you were to survive the death of your body, how might this occur?

6. If there is an all-powerful, all-good God who allows (or does not destroy) evil, do you think that God's reasons for doing so should be evident to all or most people?

NOTES

1. David Hume, *Dialogues concerning Natural Religion*, part X, ed. Kemp Smith (New York: Bobbs-Merrill, 1947), 198.

2. Sleepwalking is a rather embarrassing practice that I wrote up and published under a different name in the book *Love, Love, Love, and Other Essays*.

FIFTH CONVERSATION

Looking into Miracles, the Incarnation, Redemption,
Religious Diversity, and a Skeptical Challenge

> A genuine sense of mortality enables us to see virtue as the
> only thing of worth; and it is impossible to limit and fore-
> see the ways in which it will be required of us.
>
> —Iris Murdoch[1]

PAT: We have covered a great deal of ground. And we've also been overheard by a mutual friend, Tony, who has told me that he has a major argument addressed to all of us. But before we get to Tony, I propose a few more matters to explore. Increasingly in our debate about evil, you, Chris, seemed to appeal to what extends beyond the box (that is, the coffin). At the end of the day, I believe your form of theism involves what may be called the miraculous. For a person to survive the demise of his or her body goes beyond the natural world, as I have argued earlier. I would like to question whether it can ever be reasonable to believe in such nature-bending miracles. I would then like to critically look at specific religions. You have been defending a general theism that is neutral with respect to specific religions. After raising some specific objections against Christianity, I will raise doubts about the truth of any one religion because of the sheer multiplicity of religious faiths.

CHRIS: Very well. I assume that Tony will step in after our exchange. And I have no doubt Liz will also contribute. Let's begin with miracles.

MIRACLES

PAT: While the term "miracle" comes from the Latin term for *wonder*, it has technically come to refer to an event brought about by God or some other supernatural agent that violates or transgresses a law of nature.

CHRIS: You are correct that such a characterization of miracles came to have this technical definition, and it did so in the work of David Hume (1711–1776), but I find it very unsatisfactory for several reasons. First, the very concept of a miracle in most of Judaism, Christianity, and Islam is tied to purposive contexts in which the will or nature of God is disclosed. If we only went by the definition you offer, then God's levitating an object on some extra-solar, uninhabitable planet for a nanosecond would be a miracle if the event ran counter to the laws of gravity. This would hardly count as a miracle from a religious point of view; however, I suggest that the concept of a miracle be more explicitly linked to meaningful, valuable contexts. Second, why define a miracle as a transgression or trespass? Is it a law of nature that the Creator of the cosmos does not do specific, particular actions within the created, natural order?

PAT: It is not a recognized scientific law that God is not allowed to interfere within nature because science does not explicitly affirm or imply that there is a God who does or might interfere with the cosmos. The reason for characterizing miracles as *violations* is to capture the idea that miracles are radical breaks or irregularities in the world that cannot be caused, or are not caused, by purely natural forces. I assume that the traditional Christian belief that Jesus Christ was killed and then rose from the dead after three days is a belief in a miracle, right? If the resurrection occurred, then presumably the relevant natural laws governing bodily death were broken. Miracles have such power in religious traditions precisely because (according to believers) the events cannot be explained without bringing in a divine or some other supernatural force.

CHRIS: I do not mean to be difficult, but I still have a problem with your concept of God breaking natural laws. Let me try to reframe matters. Yes, it is true of human anatomy that if a human being is scourged and the loss of blood produces orthostatic hypotension and hypovolemic shock, the person's central ligaments are broken and so on, and then death occurs (there is a loss of all vital functions, no functioning of the brain, no circulatory and respiratory functions, and so on), the state of death will be irreversible unless some other force transfigures the person. I will not offer a detailed hypothesis of the physics of the resurrection, but I imagine that if there was a resurrection there were alterations beginning at the level of micro-particles that affected a full translation of the earthly body of Jesus into the state of glory portrayed in New Testament sources. I suggest this should still be seen not as a *breaking* or *violating*, but as an instance of God (if indeed it happened) doing something particular or specific that constitutes a divine action in history. In the miracle, something occurs that would not have occurred without God's special act.

The way I am suggesting miracles should be defined does not, by itself, either help or hinder a case for belief in miracles. But it does avoid the assumption from the beginning that there is something automatically suspect if God is brought in to explain an event. As it happens, I accept the position of most contemporary theists who hold that the cosmos is not shot through with continuous dramatic miracles (such as missing limbs being replaced in response to petitionary prayer). Still, I think many continuous, normal events occur that would not occur without special divine acts or the general will of God. Without the general creative, conserving will of God the cosmos would not exist at all or continuously, and God's character of mercy, forgiveness, grace, and justice is revealed differently through religious experience.

PAT: Let me begin with the fact that you do not hold that the occurrence of regular, dramatic, limb-growing events testifies to God's special presence. We do assume (don't we?) that the natural world is stable insofar as there are laws of nature; physical particles do not simply change their fundamental properties without some causal explanation, and the amount of matter and energy in the cosmos is conserved. Consider, now, a miracle such as a reported virgin birth, or changing water into wine, or walking on water, or dying and then rising from the dead. What evidence can be provided that these have occurred? Imagine we have widespread testimony from honest people that each of these occurred. But consider how radical such miracles would have to be! The virgin birth would have to involve parthenogenesis (from the Greek for "virgin" and "creation") and the development of an embryo without male fertilization (something we find in some plants, reptiles, and fish but not humans); turning water into wine implies a radical chemical transformation of water with fermentation; Jesus's walking on water would have to involve his body developing extraordinary buoyancy (or maybe Jesus was walking on frozen water—ice); and the resurrection would have had to involve a radical transformation of Jesus's physical constitution. Given the necessity of radical circumstances, could it ever be probable that these events occurred? I submit that it will always be more probable that the witnesses had overactive imaginations, that they had all the relevant hallucinations, or that they were self-deceived due to a mixture of a love of wonder and hope, and so on. Face it: miracles do not seem to be replicable. We do not see resurrections every day, let alone every one hundred or one thousand years. I suggest that all miracle stories will falter, the more advanced we become in science.

CHRIS: I'm not so sure. Science has led us to realize amazing cellular change that comes about in cloning. Atomic theory has led us to believe that some events are possible which we would earlier have thought preposterous. We now assume that it is possible for a person to pass through a solid wall due to the fact that matter is not dense, thus allowing for "tunneling" (the term for the quantum mechanical process by which particles can penetrate and pass through other objects). But my more general reply to you is that probability is relative to prior, independent beliefs and assumptions.

If we begin with the assumption that there is no God, the probability that miracles occur is zero. I see miracles as somewhat similar to human freedom. As an advocate of libertarian freedom, I believe we human beings are free to do one thing when we could have done otherwise. If action is genuinely free, then I think it cannot be perfectly predicted. Miracles, too, cannot be predicted perfectly, but I also think there is a type of miracle that is quite normal or routine, and that occurs in religious experience. As I argued in our third conversation, I believe that large numbers of human beings throughout recorded history have had an experiential sense, or awareness, of the divine. Human freedom and the miraculous are in the same boat, I suggest. Belief in both areas involves making a claim about what cannot be reduced to the natural and social sciences alone.

PAT: As you know, we disagree about freedom and human nature. And I also think we can explain away religious experiences in perfectly naturalistic terms. While you are right about science expanding our sense of what is possible, we are at cross-purposes on a fundamental point. Science itself has not, in all the advances you cite, given us reason to go beyond science. By claiming that someone rose from the dead or a person's cancer was miraculously cured by intercessory prayer, we do not just go beyond science, but against it. When you invoke God to explain such events you appeal to a scientifically unobservable object. Granted, you believe God is not un-experience-able but God is not thereby observable *scientifically*.

CHRIS: Let me try a different strategy. Let's return to the topic of non-human-animal conscious life. We discussed some of the difficulties in describing and assessing nonhuman-animal mental life, though we both agree that animals have some kind of consciousness. I suggest this is a defensible, sound judgment, but note that we will never directly observe scientifically the mental life of nonhuman animals. Unless one of us were to change into another species and confirm through first-person experience what it is like to be a dolphin, we will not experience dolphin psychology. This point is supported, in part, by the fact that there are still extreme behaviorists who deny dolphin and all other nonhuman-animal consciousness. These behaviorists often (but not always) grant that humans are conscious, but they vigorously affirm that there are no rationally compelling reasons to think nonhuman animals are conscious. They then wield Occam's razor: if you don't need to posit animal mental life, do not do so. I suggest rather than Occam's razor, these behaviorists are more like Procrustes (in Greek mythology, Procrustes was reputed to have a bed he would place travelers in; if the traveler was too big for the bed, Procrustes would cut the victim to match). I am all for some modest use of the razor, but one can go too far. If one were to limit our beliefs only to what is confirmable by direct observation, the behaviorists have a point, but common sense surely would see this as a procrustean maneuver. Belief in animal consciousness is overwhelmingly sensible, and yet this belief goes beyond scientific observation. I suggest that many of us who (quite sensibly) recognize animal mental life do go beyond *scientific* observation. Hence, if belief in miracles does the same, it is not ipso facto incredible. To believe in miracles, then, goes beyond science but is not against it.

PAT: I do not think the analogy works. Recognizing animal cognition and mental life in general is part of a general commonsense and scientific worldview. Animal brains and bodies have many elements in common with ours. We share a substantial genetic makeup with great apes and other animals. Human and nonhuman animals have brains and nervous systems. So, while I take your point that *as a human being* I will not experience the world the way a dolphin does, I can form a natural understanding of us and animals inhabiting the same world. Your concept of God bringing about miracles, on the other hand, involves a whole different order of being coming into the cosmos.

CHRIS: If all my arguments for the coherence of theism and reasons for believing theism is plausible and my defense of theism against your objections behind theism and defense of theism have failed, I can certainly appreciate the strength of skepticism about the miraculous. But if you think of theism as a reasonable or live option, I believe we should no more rule out the miraculous than rule out freedom or nonhuman consciousness.

LIZ: I wonder if I might get a word in at this point. I suspect this debate might come to a tie. Yes, if you have good reason to be a naturalist, you have good reason to think miracle narratives should be explained within the natural and social sciences. Conversely, if theism is reasonable, I do not see how one can automatically revert to what might be called methodological atheism—a method that rules out in principle God's special purposive activity. But while I see your debate as interesting, my concept of the divine does not hang on the reliability of miracle narratives. Why not see the miracle stories of the great world religions as metaphors or parables? Belief in the resurrection may be seen as a way to affirm the importance of resilient hope and love. Stories of a virgin birth simply celebrate the importance of a person's life. (In the ancient world, a virginal birth would be a sign of divine favor.) Stories of Jesus's producing food miraculously may be read as stories about how love can lead persons to lives of great generosity.

CHRIS: Although I am not a Christian, I think your proposal is too extreme. Yes, one might see all these stories as *also* having such metaphorical significance, but I think Christians themselves (at least the traditional ones) believe those stories reflect real historical occurrences.

LIZ: You may be right, but I see no reason why they must. After all, Christians value parables like the parable of the Good Samaritan, which commends a life of service. Why not treat the whole story of Jesus as one extensive parable?

PAT: On this point, Liz and I are on the same side. You are better off (intellectually) thinking of Jesus in terms of metaphor than as an actual incarnation of God. There is a logical problem with the incarnation.

INCARNATION AND REDEMPTION

PAT continues: You have sought to develop a self-consistent, logical concept of God, but at the very heart of Christianity there appears to be a massive contradiction. According to tradition, Jesus Christ is both God and man. Now, let's compare human and divine attributes. Consider the list:

God	Human
Necessary	Contingent
Omnipotent	Finite Power
Omniscience	Finite Knowledge
Essential Goodness	Not Essentially Good
Eternal or Everlasting	Temporal, with a Beginning and an End
Omnipresent	Finite

These properties are not complementary. They are direct contraries: if you have one property (necessity) you do not have the other (contingency). It is impossible for one person to be divine and human.

CHRIS: I do not see a problem here. There are many theories about the incarnation, but the most plausible I have heard locates the incarnation in relationship to the trinity: the idea that the Godhead contains three persons (Father, Son, and Holy Spirit) and that the incarnation involves a self-limitation of the Son. I will not take off into a massive discourse on the Trinity, but I need to get enough information in place in order to explain that while traditional Christians think Jesus is *wholly God* and *wholly man*, they do not think of Jesus as *the whole of God* or as *merely or only human*. Some Christians (in the West) tend to stress the supreme unity of the Godhead while others (in the East) tend to put more emphasis on the differentiation of persons in God. Because time is limited and all I need is just one way to show that the heart of Christianity is not a square circle, I'll choose the Eastern, more differentiated account. In this view, there is a single divine nature (consisting of necessary existence and other attributes discussed earlier), but three centers of consciousness. In a way, this is why Christians sometimes see God as the highest order of love, for in the Godhead there can be self-love, the love of another, and the love of two persons toward a third. In any event, one way to understand the incarnation is that the second member of the Trinity—the Son—undertook a radical self-limitation. The divine mind-person remains with all the divine attributes while limiting itself to what may be called a mind within a mind. Let me explain. Imagine your niece is a student in your class. As Uncle or Aunt Pat you have access to your niece's life, her background, your shared history, and so on. But in the class you must assume a role or a mind in which none of that is operative. You must limit yourself; in a similar way, the person or mind of Jesus who becomes incarnate took on a human life. He was born, thought, and had sensations through human anatomy; grew hungry, felt heat and cold with human anatomy; and so on. That limited mind (according to some Christians) became so incarnate that the incarnate child Jesus probably did not know his divine nature. Analogies other than the teacher model can be utilized. Imagine you enter a play or go to an island or adopt a new identity: we can imagine you so limiting yourself that you become wholly identified with an assumed life, or a small, focused part of your overall life. So, Jesus as an incarnate human had limited knowledge, power, and so on, but as the unincarnate member of the Godhead, Jesus retains all divine attributes.

PAT: I do not think these analogies are successful. In the case of the professor we have mere roles. And in the case of plays we have an assumed, not real, identity. Insofar as Christians believe Jesus is really divine and really human simultaneously, the contradiction remains: Jesus is both omnipotent and not omnipotent.

CHRIS: I think you do not sufficiently appreciate the kind of identification that can happen with roles, plays, and occasions of authentic self-limitation. The self-limitation and identification involved in a human incarnation would involve profound sensory, cognitive, and agentive limitations. Jesus would be subject to the appetites, desires, needs, and sensations that constitute human life. Jesus would thereby experience weakness and vulnerability.

PAT: Your portrait of the incarnation reminds me of a mental breakdown, a condition of multiple personality disorder. How can one imagine a person splitting into or containing a more limited personality or center of consciousness?

CHRIS: Maybe we are back to our first conversation about the imagination. I believe that one of the exceptional powers of the human mind is its ability to imagine a multitude of centers of consciousness. Isn't that what all good playwrights and novelists do? They seem to be able to imagine a world and then picture that world from multiple, even conflicting, points of view. Imagine a writer develops a story in which she herself is one of the characters. As one of the characters, she may have all sorts of limitations she does not have as an author. As for multiple personality disorder (MPD), psychologists currently disagree about how to understand this phenomenon in which a single subject seems able to sustain distinct personalities. I do not wish to compare the Trinity or incarnation to MPD, but the phenomena itself gives us some reason to think that a person *can* be defined by an apparently limited set of beliefs and desires that make up a distinct personality or self. The incarnation also involves a person coming to a profound self-limitation, living a human life as a human being while also not ceasing to be God.

PAT: Well, I still think your model fails and the failure is most apparent in two areas in particular: necessity and essential goodness. Let me spell this out.

I think contingency is very much at the heart of human experience. While I have deep suspicion about libertarian free will, I think most of us do (accurately) from time to time realize the vulnerability, and, ultimately, the mortality of our lives. Our mortality is deeply defined in our earliest human literature (e.g., *The Epic of Gilgamesh*, Homeric poetry). A necessarily existing being is by nature deathless. You cannot be mortal and deathless at the same time. My second objection to the incarnation involves a clash between two beliefs: God is essentially good, and Jesus was subject to temptation. If you are subject to temptation, you have to be able to sin. If Jesus is God, Jesus is essentially good. An essentially good being cannot sin. The conclusion might be complex: either God is not essentially good and Jesus was not tempted, or being tempted does not involve the ability to sin. I prefer, instead, to conclude Jesus is not (and cannot be) both God and man.

CHRIS: I will reply to both arguments. First, I agree human life is contingent (we do not necessarily exist), but is it a defining essential characteristic that we are mortal in the sense that we are annihilated at death? I doubt this. Many cultures have promoted the belief in human immortality. Were they thereby proposing that we are not human? No. But putting these cases aside, recall that Christian tradition holds that Jesus did die. So, even if mortality is a point of human nature, Jesus in fact died and yet rose.

PAT: Isn't that a contradiction in terms? Doesn't "death" mean irreversible loss of consciousness? If consciousness is regained, then there was no death.

CHRIS: I believe that if you define "death" in such a way that the person who dies perishes into nothing, then the idea that someone survives death becomes a contradiction in terms. I suggest we compromise: a person is dead if he has lost all consciousness and the natural causal foundation for consciousness (e.g., the brain cannot support the recovery of consciousness), unless there is an act of God reviving (or resurrecting) the person. Given this definition, Jesus died. As for temptations, if Jesus is God and God is essentially good, Jesus cannot do evil. Even so, to be tempted, all you may need is the desire to do something, and possibly the belief that you can do the act in question. But you may be in such a state and yet unable to do the act. Imagine you have the sort of stable character such that you could not actually steal. You may nonetheless be in a position where you genuinely are drawn to contemplate and desire stolen money.

PAT: If you really desire to steal, and the stealing is wrong, the desire to steal is wrong. Didn't Christ teach that merely lusting after another person is wrong?

CHRIS: Yes; but assume you genuinely desire the money for charitable reasons, to relieve famine, for example. You might be in a situation when your desire to steal something (to get funds for famine relief) is actually a reflection of your goodness (we would think less of you if you hadn't been tempted to steal), and yet acting on this desire would be wrong. The case of lust would be different, for I assume lust is a desire simply to use another person for the sake of one's own pleasure. As such, lust would be intrinsically wrong as a desire. But consider a related but different genuine temptation. You find Robin very attractive and think that a respectful, consensual erotic relationship with him or her would be desirable. And yet: Robin is married. Here a person might be truly tempted (desiring or longing for eros with Robin) and yet (given one's character and commitment) there would be no real possibility that adultery would occur.

PAT: Maybe you've been tempted less than most of us, but I find this heavily qualified temptation fairly weak. If I adopted some form of Christianity, I would hold that in becoming incarnate, Jesus gave up essential goodness. But there are a host of additional reasons why it is profoundly unlikely that I will come to see Christianity as a live option. Let me shift ground slightly to get at something even more basic and implausible about traditional Christianity. Most Christians believe that Christ came to rescue sinners. The idea is that sin leads to a death sentence. We all deserve death. But Jesus, as God and man, was sinless. He did not deserve to die, yet on some level or another, Jesus took our place and died our death for us. In a way, Christians believe Jesus removes our sin or guilt or the penalty for sin. This perplexing set of beliefs cries out for criticism. One can challenge parts of this picture (Does any or all sin deserve death? Has every human sinned?), but I shall go to the heart of the picture: how can guilt or punishment be transferable? If I do deserve death, how or why could the sacrifice of an innocent person remove my punishment or guilt?

CHRIS: A forceful point, but I am not as troubled with this schema. We allow for the transfer of penalties. Imagine I break a neighbor's window, confess, display remorse and so on, but I simply lack the funds to replace what I have damaged. You step in and pay on my behalf. The whole idea of transferring merit is not exclusive to Christianity. We find it also in Buddhism and, dare I say, common sense. Imagine I deserve a massive penalty, perhaps even death, and you as the magistrate are about to execute me. Imagine, too, I confess, am repentant, and beg for mercy. Perhaps I still deserve death, but then along comes a person who courageously rescued you from certain death in the past. In a sense, you owe your life to this person; she pleads for my life. Is it so odd to imagine that her merit and compassion might rightly move you to spare me?

PAT: This strikes me as altogether inappropriate and demeaning when we are thinking about justice. Imagine I do spare you, but not someone else who lacks a mediator. My mercy, then, seems capricious. Also the scenario you sketch seems to put God in the odd situation of requiring placation or appeasement. If showing mercy to you is good, I should not require intercession.

CHRIS: Maybe you do not, but maybe I need to experience the intercession in order to fully reform, be morally regenerated, repent, and repudiate my past evils.

PAT: Let's move this conversation to the whole topic of religious diversity, for that seems to be where your broadly conceived theism seems most imperiled.

RELIGIOUS DIVERSITY AND AGNOSTICISM

PAT: From the outset you have employed a capacious, open attitude toward world religions. There have indeed been periods of collaboration and tolerance between religions. But there has also been immense, sustained conflict. Religious diversity has been a source of immense strife. Christians have been anti-Semitic, launched multiple crusades, and promoted bigotry. And if conflict on earth has been bad, think of conflict about the next life. Christians have traditionally adhered to an exclusive portrait of salvation. All those not believing in Christ are going to hell. Hindus and Muslims seem locked into long-term violent strife.

CHRIS: This portrait of religious conflict is indeed damaging and in deep conflict with the founding teachings of the religions you cite. You can find texts in Christianity, Judaism, Islam, Hinduism, and Buddhism, all calling for mercy and compassion, forgiveness and reconciliation. If Jesus calls everyone to be loving, and a so-called Christian hates others, I would say this "Christian" is not a follower of Christ. As you know, I am not myself a Christian, but I do know many Christians who believe that non-Christians may be saved by Christ. They believe Christ can reach people through different means, perhaps through even an atheist tradition in which compassion is prized. I even know Christians who think Christ works to reach people after death. So, while I do not currently believe this, I do not rule it out. In short, I don't see why Christianity should be shunned on the grounds that it is narrowly exclusivist.

Today there is a great movement of interreligious cooperation. Consider, for example, the work of the Parliament of the World's Religions that adopted a common global ethic of justice, compassion, and sound stewardship in 1993. It appears to me that the diversity of religions can create a forum for dialogue and constructive exchange.

TONY: I have been following this dialogue very closely, and I compliment you both for providing good arguments. They are so good, however, that they cancel each other out. I believe the question of whether or not God exists needs to be settled like any inquiry into matters of fact. If you have equally good reason to believe X (God exists) and equally good reason not to believe X (there is no God), you should not believe either (you should be neither a theist nor an atheist). Imagine a trial in which the evidence of Robin's guilt is as strong as the counterevidence. Surely, under those circumstances, one should suspend judgment. In your debate, then, I think, because you have both done admirably, the only reasonable course of action is to adopt agnosticism. My plea for agnosticism also applies to you, Chris, in a special way. If you grant that the great religions differ (they cannot all be true on all matters), then if they are each equally justifiable, shouldn't you also be agnostic about all of them?

CHRIS: Well, let me first defend my view of world religions. I do not blend them all into one unified religious outlook, and I do recognize real differences between them. If traditional Christianity holds, then Islam is not right in denying the incarnation. But it is easy to overlook the profound similarity between religions. Each points us away from greed and narrow self-interest. With the possible exception of Taoism, most of the world religions point to something of sacred value transcending the immediate material world.

TONY: Fair enough, but I submit that insofar as all these religions have differences, it can never be justified for you to believe in one of the religions and not the others. And my broader point still holds: as long as your case for broad theism is not more compelling than Pat's case for naturalism, you ought to be neutral and withhold judgment about naturalism and theism.

PAT: Your position is intriguing, but it is not one that impacts either Chris or myself. Each of us believes that we have made a more convincing case for our different positions. Each of us also believes the other is equally intelligent, sensitive to the evidence, and so on, though I believe that the evidence supports naturalism, while Chris thinks it supports theism.

TONY: But if you appeal to the exact same evidence, don't you have to assume one of you is more intelligent or sound than the other? How can you maintain the judgment that each of you is equally intelligent, and so on?

PAT: Two points. First, we actually do not assume the exact same evidence. Chris appeals to religious experiences as evidence, whereas I think such experiences are evidentially neutral and can be explained naturalistically. Second, "intelligence" is complex. Thinking philosophically involves many resources, including science and history, logic and the imagination, and common sense and an ability to recognize, assess, and construct arguments. One person's intelligence can be displayed brilliantly in one area but not in another. My point is that the fact that you disagree with someone does not imply that on some common scale of intelligence you are smarter than your friend.

TONY: Okay, let's say you are right. My point still has considerable force. We are all part of a massive history of dialogues about God. There have been brilliant theists and brilliant atheists. If there are such extraordinary geniuses on each side, why be so confident in your own position? And what about people who have not already made up their minds? How might they even begin to think through the issues?

CHRIS: Well, someone might begin by reading a dialogue like this and checking out the afterward for more sources. These topics and arguments have never been more accessible to more people, and anyone with Internet access can find theists, naturalists, agnostics, and mystics to challenge and rethink matters. I do have two reservations, however, about your position. You seem to present agnosticism as a fallback stance; if Pat and I cannot show decisively which of our positions is more justified, then agnosticism is the only option. But this seems to bypass three points.

First, as an agnostic, I take it you not only claim that you do not know whether there is a God, you claim that we do not know either. And that is itself a fairly serious position requiring defense. Actually, as an aside, Pat and I have avoided claiming either of us *knows* we are right. Our more modest claim is that Pat, for example, believes that naturalism is true, and Pat has good reason for this. But neither of us is dogmatic and presumes the other to be *obviously wrong*. In any case, I suggest that if the arguments for and against agnosticism are of equal strength, then we should (if your thesis is correct) be agnostic about being agnostic. I personally can see a good case being made that when the evidence is equally balanced for X, belief or disbelief might be warranted. (For instance, imagine there is equally strong evidence for and against the fidelity of my friend, and yet as a friend I am fully justified to believe in his or her fidelity.)

Second, in talking about what we ought to believe or disbelieve, you are suggesting that what we believe is under our control. But that may not be right. I can't simply choose to believe that an infinite number of monkeys are in outer space typing Shakespeare's works. And there may be some beliefs I just cannot give up even in the face of powerful counter-arguments. I might, for example, run into a decisive argument by a Buddhist philosopher against the substantial existence of the self, and yet I cannot shake the belief that I exist as a concrete, enduring individual thing. But for the sake of argument, I will put aside this second assumption. Imagine I can control my beliefs, at least long-term and indirectly. Imagine the evidence is equally for and against theism *and* you are free to choose to become an atheist or theist. This brings me to a third point.

In the seventeenth century there was a philosopher and mathematician named Blaise Pascal who introduced a wager, which has come to be known as Pascal's wager. He thought that if the odds were equal whether to believe and live as if God exists or to disbelieve and live as if God does not, there are reasons to opt for theistic belief. Consider four possibilities: Imagine there is a God and you have lived as though God exists. Excellent. You have lived a life of authentic encounter with the living Creator and Redeemer. Next imagine there is no God and yet you acted as if there were. What did you lose? You perhaps wasted time in rituals, but you (presumably) lived a loving, compassionate life. Now imagine there is no God and you correctly embrace atheism. I cannot see, off hand, whether the gains are terrific. Finally, imagine there is a God and yet you are an atheist. Not good. I am NOT saying atheists cannot go to heaven and so on, but the atheist will have lost out on great goods. Now, if beliefs are not under one's immediate control, one cannot simply will to believe, but one might act as though something is true and even act on the assumption that it is true in the absence of full belief or knowledge. My point is that even if the evidence for two options is equal in weight, there can be reasons to avoid agnosticism.

PAT: I am not opposed in principle to the appeal to values in forming beliefs. When it comes to theism, I suggest that opting for naturalism makes the most sense in terms of a wager. After all, naturalism anchors you in this world, you are adopting a scientifically oriented worldview, and you avoid all the dangers associated with world religions. Consider, again,

Chris's last case: Imagine we naturalists are wrong and God exists. What sort of just God would condemn us for following our conscience and trying to follow the best evidence available? Therefore, I agree with Chris that an appeal to values can break an evidential tie, even though I believe that a robust appeal to values will show atheism to be preferable to theism. Instead of Pascal's wager, I recommend a wager for naturalism. I only regret that this wager will probably never be called Pat's wager.

CHRIS: I'll call it Pat's wager, dear friend. While I believe the values cut the other way, I do want to respond to your point about God and following one's conscience. I could not accept a form of theism that holds that God condemns a person who seeks a life of virtue and whose honest reflection leads him or her to think there is no God.

PAT: Let me return this compliment: while I remain unpersuaded by your arguments, as an atheist I do not condemn someone like yourself whose honest reflection leads him or her to (the mistaken view of) theism.

CHRIS: I love you.

PAT: I love you, too.

TONY: Settle down, both of you! And don't forget the virtues of agnosticism. I suppose one might be a dogmatic agnostic, but one may also adopt agnosticism as an exercise of humility and wisdom. In the ancient world, some of the greatest agnostics or skeptics were opposed to slavery and political violence. Doubt about both naturalism *and* theism can also open one up to a third or fourth option. After all, our conversation has only taken on theism and naturalism. We might talk about a host of alternative models of God or forms of naturalism that support spiritual values. We should also explore traditional and contemporary Buddhist concepts of the self. Additionally, I have a few arguments of my own with respect to theism and atheism that I *have* to bring up.

LIZ: Very well, then. Let's start over from the beginning, with an ever-widening format.

CHRIS, PAT, and TONY: You're on!

QUESTIONS FOR FURTHER INQUIRY

1. Must a scientist rule out the possibility of miracles? If so, is the scientific method essentially atheistic or agnostic? Are miracles indispensable to religion?
2. When, if ever, might the sacrifice or virtue of a good person remove or alleviate the guilt or punishment of a wrongdoer?
3. In U.S. criminal court trials, an accused person is to be considered innocent until proven guilty. Is there a parallel principle at work with respect to theism or atheism?
4. Consider cases other than religious ones in which a Pascalian wager argument has a plausible role.

NOTE

1. Iris Murdoch, *The Sovereignty of the Good* (New York: Schocken Books, 1971), 99.

AFTERWORD

Sources for Dialogues about God *and Some Suggested Further Reading*

Pat the naturalist is a blend of different philosophers, including Richard Dawkins, Daniel Dennett, Kai Nielson, Paul Edwards, Simon Blackburn, and others. The argument for the incoherence of theism on the grounds that a disembodied mind is incoherent can be found in work by Anthony Kenny, Paul Edwards, Antony Flew, Bede Rundle, and others. Pat's case against the coherence of theistic attributes is based on works by Michael Martin. The objections to theistic arguments and the case against theism based on evil comes from John Schellenberg, Paul Draper, Dale Jacquette, Michal Martin, William Rowe, Bertrand Russell, Matthew Bagger, Graham Oppy, and others. All the above, especially Michal Martin, are behind Pat's more specific objections and arguments in the last chapter. Pat's personality or character is a blend of those who contributed to *Philosophers without God*, edited by Louise Antony (New York: Oxford University Press, 2007).

Chris's theism is derived from Richard Swinburne, Alvin Plantinga, Nicholas Wolterstorff, Robert Adams, Marilyn Adams, Linda Zazebski, William Hasker, Stewart Goetz, Richard Purtill, and T. V. Morris, among other contemporary philosophers, and from earlier twentieth-century writers: A. E. Taylor, C. A. Campbell, F. R. Tennant, A. C. Ewing, and H. D. Lewis. Chris's personality or character is a blend of some of those who contributed to *God and the Philosophers*, edited by T. V. Morris (New York: Oxford University Press, 1996), and Kelly J. Clark's *Philosophers Who Believe* (Downers Grove, Ill.: InterVarsity Press, 1997).

Liz is inspired (in part) by Brian Davies, but she is particularly modeled after many students at my college, especially Elizabeth Duel.

Davies's work is highly recommended as the best alternative to Chris's form of theism, according to which God is personal or person-like. Davies defends the goodness of God while arguing that such goodness should not be understood in terms of the goodness of moral agency.

Tony is modeled after the great skeptic Sextus Empiricus, and some contemporary agnostics like Anthony Kenny.

For further reading, you can make use of free online access to *The Stanford Encyclopedia of Philosophy*, which features good references for philosophy of religion. I have co-edited the Blackwell *Companion to the Philosophy of Religion* and *Philosophy of Religion: A Reader*, which may also be of interest. See also the superb *Routledge Companion to Philosophy of Religion*, edited by Chad Meister and Paul Copan, and *The Oxford Handbook of Philosophy of Religion*, edited by William Wainwright. For an overview of the philosophical history of thinking about God and religion in the modern era, see my *Evidence and Faith: Philosophy and Religion since the Seventeenth Century*.

ABOUT THE AUTHOR

Charles Taliaferro (Ph.D., Brown; MTS, Harvard) is a professor of philosophy at St. Olaf College. He has taught at the University of Massachusetts, Brown University, and the University of Notre Dame. He has lectured on philosophy of religion at Oxford, Cambridge, Princeton, Yale, NYU, St. Andrews University (Scotland), University of Chicago, Beijing University (China), and elsewhere, and he has been a Visiting Scholar at Oxford University and Columbia University. He is on the editorial board of *Religious Studies*, *Sophia*, *Faith and Philosophy*, *Philosophy Compass*, *Ars Disputandi*, and the *American Philosophical Quarterly*. Taliaferro has authored six books, most recently *Evidence and Faith: Philosophy and Religion since the Seventeenth Century*. He is the co-editor of the Blackwell *Companion to the Philosophy of Religion*. He is currently working on religious pluralism and tolerance, and the debate between theism and naturalism. Taliaferro enjoys contributing to Open Court's books on philosophy and popular culture, and he has authored a book of forty essays on the topic of love, entitled *Love, Love, Love, and Other Essays*.